RHYMNEY AND NEW TREDEGAR LINES

Vic Mitchell and Keith Smith

Front cover: The Rhymney Railway used almost entirely tank locomotives. No. 47 was one of a batch built for it by Sharp Stewart in 1884. (P.Q.Treloar coll.)

Back cover: Locomotive haulage returned at peak times for several years until 2006. No. 47712 departs from Bargoed at 17.15 on 5th June 1996, bound for Rhymney. (B.Robbins)

Published April 2009

ISBN 978 1 906008 48 2

Design Deborah Esher
Typesetting Barbara Mitchell

Published by
Middleton Press
Easebourne Lane
Midhurst
West Sussex
GU29 9AZ
Tel: 01730 813169
Fax: 01730 812601
Email: info@middletonpress.co.uk
www.middletonpress.co.uk

Printed in the United Kingdom by Henry Ling Limited, at the Dorset Press, Dorchester, DT1 1HD

CONTENTS

INDEX

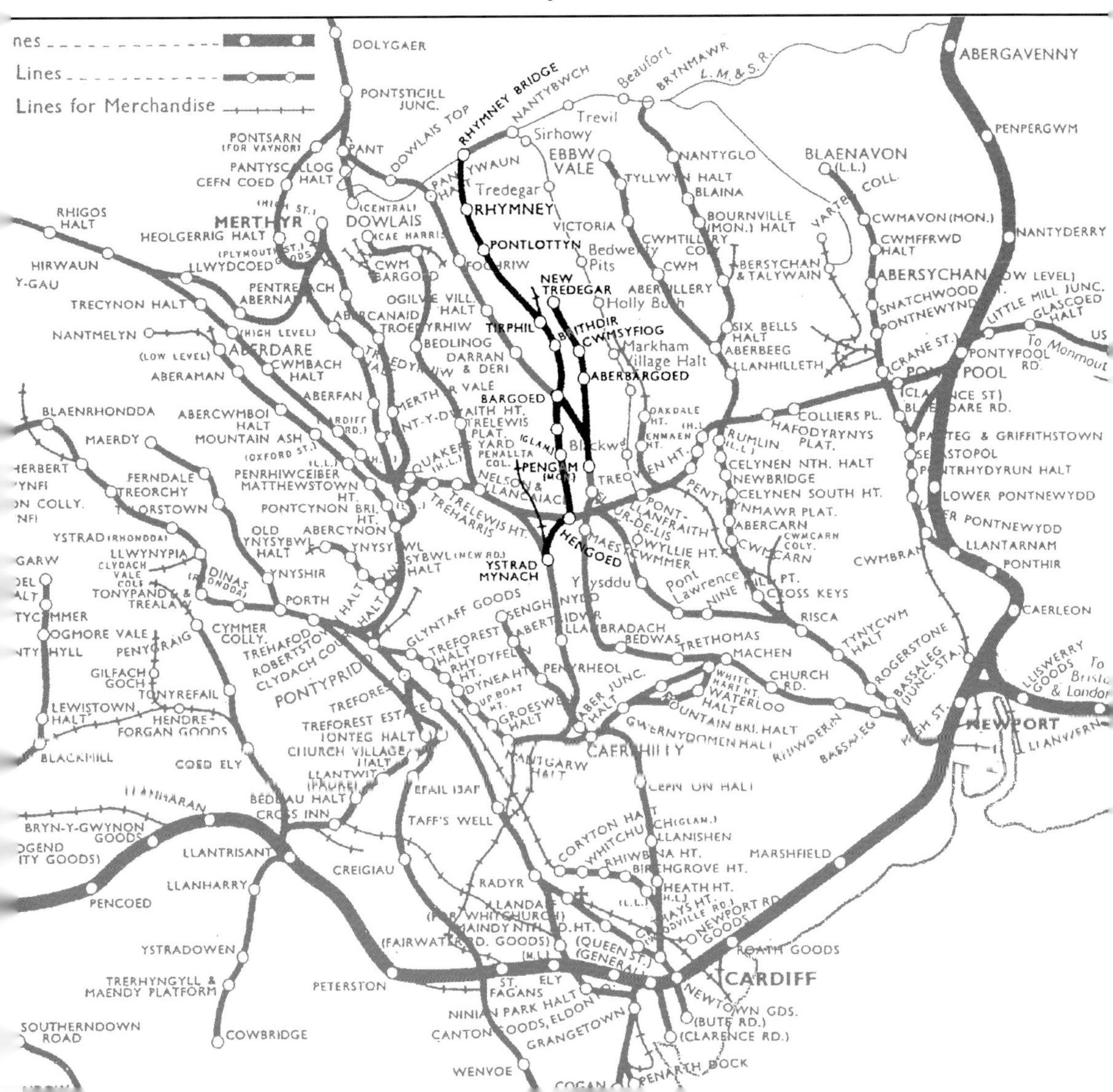

I. GWR map for 1947.

ACKNOWLEDGEMENTS

We are very grateful for the assistance received from many of those mentioned in the credits also to A.R.Carder, R.Caston, L.Crosier, G.Croughton, A.Dukes, N.Langridge, B.Lewis, C.G.Maggs, Mr D. and Dr S.Salter, S.Vincent, T.Walsh and especially our always supportive wives, Barbara Mitchell and Janet Smith.

GEOGRAPHICAL SETTING

Our journeys are in the upper part of the Rhymney Valley and the lines were built on opposite sides of the Rhymney River. They were thus in Glamorganshire and Monmouthshire, also in different countries at that time.

The steep sided valley contained numerous very productive coal mines. Some were of great depth, being in the central part of the coal basin.

At the head of the valley, the western line climbed onto the almost treeless and infertile upland, which leads to the Brecon Beacons. Iron mining and production was once important in the Rhymney area.

The maps are to the scale of 25ins to 1 mile with north at the top, unless otherwise indicated.

Note: Welsh spelling and hyphenation has varied over the years and so we have generally used the most recent form, as have the railways.

II. Gradient profile for the west route. The eastern one to Rhymney Lower was similar. The mileage starts at 14 and ends at 25.

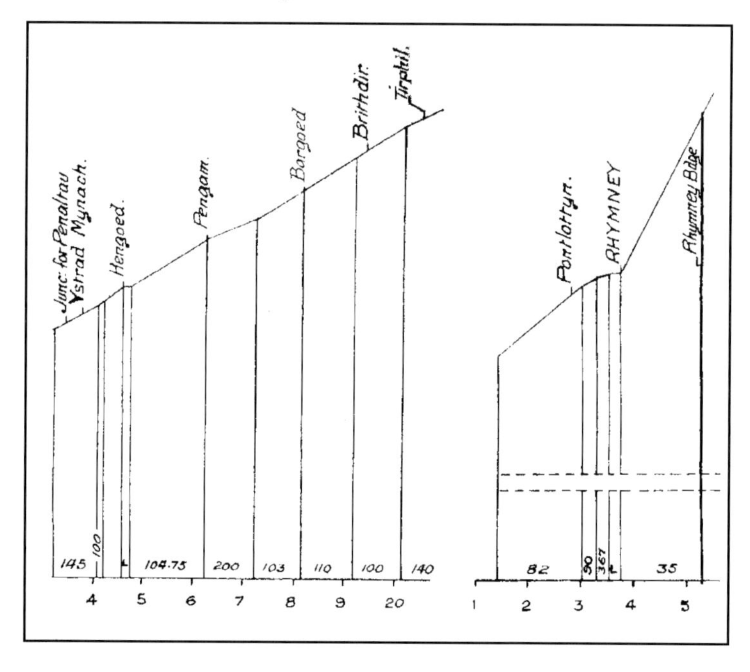

HISTORICAL BACKGROUND

The Rhymney Railway received its Act on 24th July 1854 and it became the first conventional railway in the area when it opened for freight traffic on 25th March 1858. Passenger service began on 30th March of that year, trains originating at Cardiff. It opened a branch northwest from Bargoed to Deri in 1864. It was two miles long and carried freight.

The Brecon & Merthyr Railway extended its passenger operation south when services between Pant (north of Merthyr) and Pengam began on 1st August 1868. These trains traversed RR tracks, on the western flank, between Deri and Bargoed, also for ½ mile south thereof. Its route north from Pengam to Rhymney was on the Monmouthshire side of the Rhymney Valley and it opened in 1866 for freight and passengers on 16th April of that year.

The line along the Heads of the Valleys was largely a London & North Western Railway creation in 1862-73. However, the section between Nantybwch and Rhymney Bridge was a joint LNWR/RR operation, as was the Rhymney Bridge-Rhymney link. Both parts opened on 5th September 1871. The LNWR had running powers over the RR to Cardiff Docks.

The RR and the B&MR were absorbed into the Great Western Railway in 1922 and the LNWR became part of the London Midland & Scottish Railway in 1923. The section north of Rhymney was subsequently a GWR/LMS joint line. The running powers to Cardiff were ended in 1930 by a pooling arrangement.

Nationalisation in 1948 resulted in the GWR forming the Western Region and the LMS becoming the London Midland Region of British Railways. However the Rhymney-Rhymney Bridge section became entirely WR responsibility.

Passenger service withdrawals began on 14th April 1930 with the former B&MR stations at Rhymney (Lower) and Abertysswg. Rhymney-Rhymney Bridge followed on 23rd September 1953 and Pengam (Mon.) to New Tredegar succumbed on 31st December 1962, along with the remainder of the former B&MR. Freight withdrawals are given in the captions.

This left trains running from Cardiff to Rhymney. Following privatisation they were operated by the Cardiff Railway Co. Ltd (Prism Rail plc) from 13th October 1996. Trains had been branded "Valley Lines" since 1985. The services were run by Wales & Borders from November 2001. The operator was Arriva Trains Wales from 7th December 2003.

PASSENGER SERVICES

Cardiff - Rhymney

The initial timetable showed two trains daily, but an extra one on weekdays was added after three weeks. This frequency still applied in 1876, but by 1893 the figures were seven on weekdays and two on Sundays. By 1910, the frequency had risen to 14 and 4 and in 1935 it was 21 and 4. Some LNWR through coaches ran over the route until 1916.

Wartime reduction meant only 12 and 2 ran the full length in 1943, but by 1955 it was back to 25 and 8. The 1963 timetable showed 24 and 11. A regular interval service had started in the Autumn of 1953. A 15 minute interval timetable to Bargoed started in January 2006.

Down trains run away from London on most lines, but in the Welsh Valleys herein they run downhill to the coast.

Newport to New Tredegar

Almost all trains started at Newport and ran through to the terminus at Rhymney (Lower) until services were cut back to New Tredegar in 1930. No Sunday trains have been found.

There were three or four trains until about 1905 on weekdays and seven or eight into the 1930s. Then eleven reducing to nine at closure were the norm.

Man., Cornelius Lundie.] **RHYMNEY.** [Sec. John B. Shand.

Fares.			All Class.	Week Days.			Sundays.		Up.	Week Days.			Sundays.	
1 cl.	2 cl.	3 cl.	Down.	mrn	aft	aft	mrn	aft	Adam St. Sta.	mrn	aft	aft	mrn	aft
s. d.	s. d.	s. d.	Rhymney ...dep	8 15	2 30	5 40	8 0	4 10	Cardiff ....dep	8 0	1245	5 30	9 40	5 5[illegible]
0 2	0 1½	0 1	Pontlottyn	8 19	2 34	5 44	8 4	4 16	WalnutTree B.	8 18	1 3	5 48	9 58	6 1[illegible]
0 8	0 6	0 3	Tir Phil	8 27	2 40	5 5[illegible]	8 10	4 24	Caerphilly	8 30	1 10	5 56	10 6	6 2[illegible]
1 0	0 9	0 5½	Bargoed 130 ..	8 35	2 48	6 0	8 18	4 32	Ystrad ....[24	8 42	1 24	6 8	1036	6 3[illegible]
1 4	1 0	0 7	Pengam 127	8 40	2 52	6 6	8 25	4 42	Hengoed 26 { a	8 50	1 28	6 12	....	....
1 6	1 3	0 9	Hengoed 26 { a	8 50	....	6 10	....	....	WestMid.J. { d	1010	1 3[illegible]	6 17	1020	6 4[illegible]
			West Mid J. { dp	10[illegible]	2 57	6 15	8 30	4 50	Pengam	1016	1 40	6 22	1025	6 4[illegible]
1 10	1 4	0 10	Ystrad	1014	3 0	6 [illegible]	8 34	4 54	Bargoed 130	1025	1 47	6 27	1035	6 5[illegible]
2 6	1 10	1 2½	Caerphilly	1022	[illegible] 10	6 34	8 44	5 8	Tir Phil	1032	1 53	6 34	1043	7 [illegible]
3 2	2 4	1 6	Walnut Tree Br.	1037	3 17	6 4[illegible]	8 52	5 17	Pontlottyn	1040	2 0	6 4[illegible]	1051	7 1[illegible]
4 [illegible]	[illegible]	[illegible]	Cardiff	[illegible]	3 35	[illegible]	9 10	5 35	Rhymney ..arr	1045	2 5	6 47	1055	7 1[illegible]

June 1869

December 1895

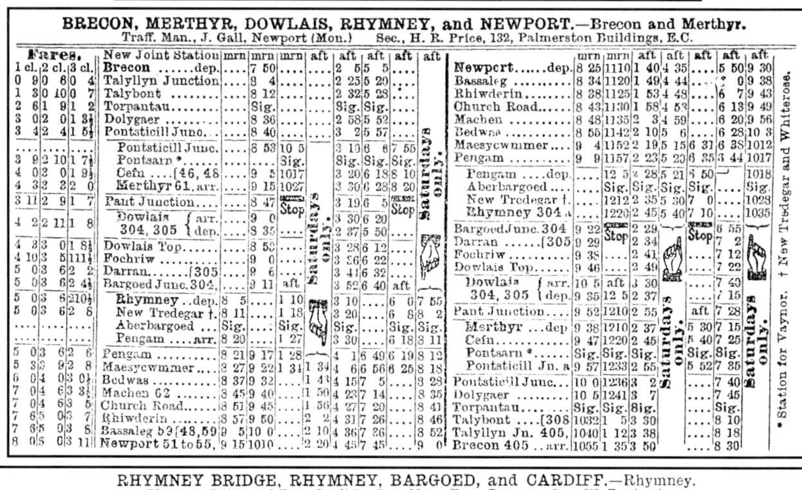

BRECON, MERTHYR, DOWLAIS, RHYMNEY, and NEWPORT.—Brecon and Merthyr.
Traff. Man., J. Gall, Newport (Mon.) Sec., H. R. Price, 132, Palmerston Buildings, E.C.

Fares.			New Joint Station	mrn	mrn	mrn	aft	aft	aft	aft	aft
1 cl.	2 cl.	3 cl.	Brecon ......dep.	....	7 50	....	....	2 5	5 5	....	
0 9	0 6	0 4	Talyllyn Junction	....	8 4	....	....	2 25	5 20	....	
1 3	0 10	0 7	Talybont	....	8 12	....	....	2 32	5 28	....	
2 6	1 9	1 2	Torpantau	....	Sig.	....	....	Sig.	Sig.	....	
3 0	2 0	1 3½	Dolygaer	....	8 36	....	....	2 58	5 52	....	
3 4	2 4	1 5½	Pontsticill Junc.	....	8 40	....	....	3 2	5 57	....	
....	....	....	Pontsticill Junc.	....	8 53	10 5	Saturdays only.	3 16	6 7	7 55	Saturdays only.
3 9	2 10	1 7½	Pontsarn *	....	Sig.	Sig.		Sig.	Sig.	Sig.	
4 0	2 0	1 9½	Cefn ....[46, 48	....	9 5	1017		3 20	6 18	8 10	
4 3	2 2	2 0	Merthyr 61.arr.	....	9 15	1027		3 30	6 28	8 20	
3 11	2 9	1 7	Pant Junction	....	8 47	Stop		3 19	6 5	Stop	
4 2	2 11	1 8	Dowlais { arr.	....	9 0			3 30	6 20		
			304, 305 { dep.	....	8 35			2 37	5 50		
4 3	3 0	1 8½	Dowlais Top	....	8 53			3 28	6 12		
4 10	3 5	1 11½	Fochriw	....	9 0			3 36	6 22		
5 0	3 6	2 2	Darran......[305	....	9 6			3 41	6 32		
5 0	3 6	2 4½	Bargoed Junc. 304	....	9 11	aft		3 52	6 40	aft	
5 0	3 6	2 10½	Rhymney ..dep.	8 5	....	1 10		3 10	....	6 0	7 55
5 0	3 6	2 6	New Tredegar †.	8 11	....	1 18		3 20	....	6 8	8 2
....	....	....	Aberbargoed	Sig.	....	Sig.		Sig.	....	Sig.	Sig.
....	....	....	Pengam ....arr.	8 20	....	1 27		3 30	....	6 18	8 11
5 0	3 6	2 6	Pengam	8 21	9 17	1 28	....	4 1	6 49	6 19	8 12
5 3	3 9	2 8	Maesycwmmer	8 27	9 22	1 34	1 34	4 6	6 56	6 25	8 18
6 0	4 0	3 0½	Bedwas	8 37	9 32	....	1 43	4 15	7 5	....	8 28
7 0	4 6	3 3½	Machen 62	8 45	9 40	....	1 50	4 23	7 14	....	8 35
7 0	4 6	3 5	Church Road	8 51	9 45	....	1 56	4 27	7 20	....	8 41
7 6	5 0	3 7	Rhiwderin	8 57	9 50	....	2 2	4 31	7 26	....	8 46
7 6	5 0	3 5	Bassaleg 59[48,59	9 5	10 0	....	2 10	4 36	7 26	....	8 52
8 0	5 0	3 11	Newport 51 to 55	9 15	1010	....	2 20	4 45	7 45	....	9 0

	mrn	mrn	aft	aft	aft	aft	aft
Newport......dep.	8 25	1110	1 40	4 35	....	5 50	9 30
Bassaleg	8 34	1120	1 49	4 44	....	[illegible] 0	9 38
Rhiwderin........	8 38	1125	1 53	4 48	....	6 7	9 43
Church Road......	8 43	1130	1 58	4 53	....	6 13	9 49
Machen	8 48	1135	2 3	4 59	....	6 20	9 56
Bedwas	8 55	1142	2 10	5 6	....	6 28	10 3
Maesycwmmer....	9 4	1152	2 19	5 15	6 31	6 38	1012
Pengam	9 9	1157	2 23	5 20	6 35	6 44	1017
Pengam ....dep.	....	12 5	2 28	5 21	6 50	—	1018
Aberbargoed	....	Sig.	Sig.	Sig.	Sig.	....	Sig.
New Tredegar †.	....	1212	2 35	5 30	7 0	....	1028
Rhymney 304 a	....	1220	2 45	5 40	7 10	....	1035
Bargoed Junc. 304	9 22	Stop	2 29	Saturdays only.	Stop	6 55	Saturdays only.
Darran ......[305	9 29		2 34			7 2	
Fochriw	9 38		2 41			7 12	
Dowlais Top......	9 46		2 49			7 22	
Dowlais { arr.	10 5	aft	3 30		....	7 40	
304, 305 { dep.	9 35	12 5	2 37		....	7 15	
Pant Junction....	9 52	1210	2 55		aft	7 28	
Merthyr ...dep	9 38	1210	2 37		5 30	7 15	
Cefn	9 47	1220	2 45		5 40	7 25	
Pontsarn *	Sig.	Sig.	Sig.		Sig.	Sig.	
Pontsticill Jn. a	9 57	1233	2 55		5 52	7 35	
Pontsticill Junc...	10 0	1236	3 2		....	7 40	
Dolygaer	10 5	1241	3 7		....	7 45	
Torpantau	Sig.	Sig.	Sig.		....	Sig.	
Talybont ....[308	1032	1 5	3 30		....	8 10	
Talyllyn Jn. 405.	1040	1 12	3 38		....	8 18	
Brecon 405 ..arr.	1055	1 35	3 50		....	8 30	

* Station for Vaynor. † New Tredegar and Whiterose.

RHYMNEY BRIDGE, RHYMNEY, BARGOED, and CARDIFF.—Rhymney.
Rhymney Railway Offices, Cardiff. Gen. Man., E. A. Prosser. Sec., W. Fairlamb.

Miles	Down.	mrn	mrn	mrn	mrn	mrn	mrn	aft	aft	aft (Saturdays only)	aft (Except Saturdays)	aft	aft (Z Sats. only)	aft	aft	aft	aft	aft	aft	aft	Sundays mrn	aft	aft	aft
	Rhymney Bridge..dep.	6 30	7 33	....	9 0	10 5	11 20	....	....			1 50		2 45	4 6	4 50	6 25	....	8 15	1010	....	....	....	....
1¼	Rhymney 463	6 35	7 41	8 50	9 6	10 g 33	11 27	1225	1 5			1 56		2 51	4 20	4 57	6 35	7 g 0	8 20	1015	9 0	1155	....	5 5
2¼	Pontlottyn ¶	6 39	7 45	8 g 55	9 10	10 g 37	11 32	1229	1 9			2 0		2 55	4 24	5 2	6 40	7 g 5	8 25	1019	9 5	12 0	....	5 10
5	Tir Phil & New Tredegar	6 45	7 51	9 g 3	9 17	10 g 45	11 38	1235	1 15			2 8		3 1	4 30	5 10	6 46	7 g 11	8 31	1025	9 10	12 7	....	5 15
6	Brithdir	6 49	7 55	9 g 7	9 21	10 g 49	11 42	1239	1 19			2 12		3 5	4 34	5 14	6 51	7 g 17	8 35	1029	9 14	1211	....	5 19
7½	Bargoed † ¶ 463	6 53	8 0	9 g 11	9 25	10 g 53	11 47	1244	1 24			2 16	2 g 33	3 14	4 39	5 19	6 58	7 g 21	8 40	1033	9 18	1215	....	5 23
9	Pengam	6 58	8 5	9 g 18	9 30	11 g 0	11 52	1249	1 28			2 22	2 g 45	3 19	4 43	5 26	7 4	7 g 28	8 45	1037	9 23	1220	....	5 28
10½	Hengoed ‡ 67	7 3	8 11	9 g 23	9 35	11 g 5	11 57	1254	1 33			2 28	2 g 50	3 24	4 48	5 31	7 10	7 g 33	8 50	1042	9 31	1225	....	5 36
11½	Ystrad Mynach 484	7 6	8 15	[illegible]	9 38	11 11	12 0	1257	1 36			2 32	2 g 53	3 29	4 54	5 37	7 17	[illegible]	8 55	1045	9 35	1228	....	5 40
14½	Llanbradach	7 12	8 21	....	9 45	11 18	12 7	1 8	1 43			2 46	2 g 59	3 36	5 12	5 43	7 24	[illegible]	9 2	1052	9 40	1234	....	5 45
17	Caerphilly 63	7 18	8 27	9 45	9 51	11 25	12 13	1 15	1 50		1 59	2 52	3 9	3 45	5 19	5 49	7 30	8 45	[illegible]	1058	9 46	1240	4 0	5 51
20½	Llanishen ..[103 to 107	7 27	8 38	....	9 59	11 34	12 22	1 24	1 59		2 8	3 1	3 19	3 53	5 29	5 59	7 39	8 54	9 19	11 8	9 55	1249	4 9	6 0
24	Cardiff § 54 to 61, 89.	7 33	8 44	9 58	10 5	11 40	12 28	1 30	2 5		2 14	3 7	3 25	4 0	5 35	6 5	7 45	9 0	9 25	1115	10 0	1255	4 15	6 5

Mls	Rhymney Station.	mrn	mrn	mrn	mrn	mrn	aft	aft (Except Sats)	aft (Except Saturdays)	aft (Sats. only)	aft	aft	aft	aft	aft	aft	aft	aft	aft	Sundays mrn	aft	aft	aft
—	Cardiff............dep.	5 40	7 45	8 35	9 18	1050	1210	1 10	1 20	2 10	3 5	4 10	5 27	6 5	7 15	8 10	9 c 15	10 s 10	11 0	1030	3 0	8 35	....
3½	Llanishen	5 48	7 52	8 43	9 26	1058	1217	1 17	1 27	2 18	3 13	4 18	5 35	6 13	7 22	8 18	9 c 22	10 s 17	11 7	1037	3 7	8 42	....
7	Caerphilly 63	5 56	8 0	8 51	9 35	11 6	1226	1 24	1 35	2 25	3 21	4 26	5 42	6 21	7 30	8 26	9 c 30	10 s 25	1115	1045	3 15	8 50	....
9½	Llanbradach	6 2	8 6	8 58	9 41	1113	1232		1 g 54	2 31	3 27	4 33	5 48	6 27	7 36	8 32	9 c 36	10 s 32	1122	1051	....	8 56	....
12½	Ystrad Mynach	6 8	8 12	9 5	9 49	1121	1238	1 g 20	2 g 1	2 37	3 g 40	4 40	6 g 0	6 33	7 g 50	8 38	9 c 43	10 s 39	1128	1056	....	9 2	....
13½	Hengoed ‡ 67	6 12	8 25	9 9	9 g 55	1129	1242	1 g 25	2 g 4	2 43	3 g 43	4 44	6 g 4	6 37	7 g 53	8 44	9 c 47	10 s 44	1133	11 5	....	9 6	....
15	Pengam ¶	6 17	8 30	9 14	10 g 0	1133	1247	1 g 30	2 g 9	2 53	3 g 48	4 49	6 g 9	6 42	7 g 59	8 49	9 c 52	10 s 48	1138	11 9	....	9 11	....
16½	Bargoed † 463	6 23	8 36	9 24	10 g 5	1142	1255	1 g 35	2 g 15	2 59	3 g 53	4 55	6 g 16	6 48	8 g 6	8 55	9 c 58	10 s 53	1144	1114	....	9 16	....
18	Brithdir	6 27	8 40	9 29	10 g 9	1146	1259	1 g 39		3 3	3 g 57	5 0	6 g 20	6 52	8 g 10	8 59	10 c 2	10 s 58	1149	1118	....	9 21	....
19	Tir Phil & New Tredegar	6 31	8 44	9 33	10 g 13	1150	1 4	1 g 43		3 7	4 g 1	5 5	6 g 24	6 57	8 g 14	9 4	10 c 6	11 s 2	1154	1122	....	9 24	....
21½	Pontlottyn ¶	6 38	8 51	9 40	10 g 20	1155	1 10	1 g 50		3 13	4 g 8	5 11	6 g 32	7 3	8 g 22	9 11	10 c 12	11 s 8	12 0	1128	....	9 30	....
22½	Rhymney 463	6 48	8 54	9 46	10 45	12 0	1 19	1 g 53		3 16	4 20	5 20	6 g 36	7 13	8 g 26	9 23	10 c 16	11 s 15	12 7	1132	....	9 33	....
24	RhymneyBdg. 456 arr.	6 54	....	9 53	10 51	....	1 25	....		3 26	4 26	5 27	....	7 20	....	9 30	....	....	s 1212	....	....	....	....

NOTES.

b Thursdays and Saturdays.
c Thursdays only.
g Motor Car, one class only.
s Saturdays only.
† Bargoed and Aber Bargoed.
‡ Hengoed and Maesycwmmer.
§ Above ¼ mile to G.W. Station.
¶ "Halts" at Troedyrhiwfuwch, between Pontlottyn and Tir-Phil and New Tredegar; Gilfach Fargoed, between Bargoed and Aber Bargoed and Pengam.

March 1909

November 1930

Miles.	Down.	mrn	mrn	mrn	mrn	mrn	mrn	mrn	mrn	mrn S	mrn	Through Train from Pontypool Road, see page 82.	aft S	aft S	aft S	aft E	aft S	aft E	aft	aft	aft X	aft S	aft E
	Rhymney Bridge...dep.	5 40	..	..	7 30	8 12	9 0	9 30	..	..	11 35		..	..	..	..	..	1 53	2 10	3 40	..	..	..
1¼	Rhymney 87	5 46	..	..	7 40	8 19	9 10	9 35	..	1133	11 47		..	..	1 0	1 5	..	2 0	2 21	3 55	..	4 10	4 20
2¼	Pontlottyn	5 51	..	..	7 45	8 24	9 15	..	..	1140	11 52		..	..	1 5	1 10	..	2 5	2 26	4 1	..	4 15	4 25
4¾	Tir Phil	5 59	..	..	7 53	8 32	9 23	..	..	1149	12 0		..	..	1 13	1 18	..	2 13	2 34	4 9	..	4 23	4 33
6	Brithdir	6 3	..	..	7 57	8 36	9 27	..	..	1154	12 5		..	..	1 17	1 22	..	2 17	2 38	4 13	..	4 27	4 37
7	Bargoed ¶ 86, 87	6 9	..	7 42	8 4	8 41	9 34	..	..	12 3	12 12		..	1 14	1 23	1 28	..	2 23	2 43	4 20	..	4 30	4 40
9	Pengam (Glam.)	6 15	..	7 48	8 10	8 48	9 40	..	..	1210	12 18		..	1 20	1 29	1 34	..	2 29	2 49	4 26	..	..	..
10¾	Hengoed G 82, 84 { arr.	6 19	..	7 52	8 14	8 52	9 44	..	..	1214	12 22		..	1 24	1 33	1 38	..	2 33	2 56	4 30	..	..	..
	{ dep.	6 20	..	7 53	8 18	8 58	9 46	..	..	1217	12 27		..	1 29	1 35	1 40	..	2 35	3 1	4 31	4 45	..	..
11½	Ystrad Mynach	6 24	..	7 57	8 22	9 2	9 50	..	..	1222	12 31		1 2	1 33	1 39	1 44	..	2 39	3 5	4 35	4 49	..	..
14½	Llanbradach	6 30	7 2	8 4	8 29	9 9	9 57	..	..	..	12 38		1 9	1 40	1 46	1 51	..	2 46	3 12	4 42	4 56	..	..
17	Caerphilly ¶ 82, 85b, 87b { arr.	..	7 8	8 10	8 35	9 15	10 3	..	..	..	12 44		1 15	1 46	1 52	1 57	..	2 52	3 18	4 48	5 2	..	..
	{ dep.	..	7 10	8 12	8 37	9 18	10 6	..	11 0	..	12 47		1 18	1 50	1 56	2 2	2 15	..	3 22	4 50	..	..	..
20½	Llanishen ¶ |73, 92 to 95	..	7 20	8 22	8 45	9 28	1014	..	1110	..	12 55		1 26	..	2 4	2 10	2 25	..	3 32	4 58	..	..	..
24	Cardiff H 62, 67, arr.	..	7 29	8 31	8 52	9 37	1023	..	1119	1247	1 4		1 33	2 5	2 11	2 17	2 35	..	3 41	5 7	..	..	..

Down.	Week Days—*Continued.* aft S	aft	aft	aft S	aft	aft S		aft	aft	aft S	aft					Sundays. mrn		aft	aft	aft	aft	aft	aft
Rhymney Bridge...dep.	..	..	..	..	5 45	6 50	..	7 30	8 45	..	10 15	..	..	..	..	..	..	..	..	..	..	..	..
Rhymney 87	4 40	..	..	..	5 55	6 56	..	7 40	8 52	9 40	10 22	..	..	..	..	10 0	..	..	..	4 0	..	8 30	..
Pontlottyn	4 45	..	..	..	6 0	7 1	..	7 45	8 57	9 45	10 27	..	..	..	..	10 5	..	..	..	4 5	..	8 35	..
Tir Phil	4 53	..	..	..	6 8	7 9	..	7 53	9 5	9 53	10 35	..	..	..	..	1013	..	..	..	4 13	..	8 43	..
Brithdir	4 57	..	..	..	6 12	7 13	..	7 57	9 9	9 57	10 39	..	..	..	..	1017	..	..	..	4 17	..	8 47	..
Bargoed ¶ 86, 87	5 1	..	..	5 46	6 17	7 20	..	8 2	9 16	10 2	10 45	..	..	..	..	1022	..	..	..	4 22	..	8 54	..
Pengam (Glam.)	5 7	..	..	5 52	6 25	7 26	..	8 8	9 22	10 8	10 51	..	..	..	..	1028	..	..	..	4 28	..	9 0	..
Hengoed G 82, 84 { arr.	5 11	..	..	5 56	6 29	7 30	..	8 12	9 26	1012	10 55	..	..	..	..	1032	..	..	..	4 32	..	9 4	..
{ dep.	5 12	..	..	5 57	6 32	7 32	..	8 21	9 28	1017	11 0	..	..	..	..	1040	..	..	..	4 34	..	9 10	..
Ystrad Mynach	5 15	..	..	6 1	6 36	7 36	..	8 25	9 32	1021	11 4	..	..	..	..	1044	..	..	..	4 38	..	9 14	..
Llanbradach	..	..	..	6 8	6 43	7 43	..	8 32	9 39	1028	11 11	..	..	..	..	1051	..	..	..	4 45	..	9 21	..
Caerphilly ¶ 82, 85b, 87b { arr.	..	..	..	6 14	6 50	7 49	..	8 39	9 47	1034	11 17	..	..	..	..	1057	..	..	..	4 51	..	9 27	..
{ dep.	..	5 22	6 5	6 17	6 52	7 52	..	8 41	9 50	1037	11 20	..	..	..	..	11 0	..	1 45	3 30	4 53	5 35	9 28	1050
Llanishen ¶ |73, 92 to 95	..	5 32	6 13	..	7 2	8 0	..	8 51	10 0	1045	11 28	..	..	..	..	1110	..	1 55	3 40	5 3	5 45	9 38	..
Cardiff H 62, 67, arr.	..	5 41	6 22	6 32	7 11	8 7	..	9 0	10 9	1054	11 35	..	..	..	..	1119	..	2 4	3 49	5 12	5 54	9 47	11 5

E Except Saturdays.
G Hengoed (Low Level) adjoins High Level and about ½ mile to Maesycwmmer Station.
H Queen St; over ½ mile to General.
m Rail Motor Car, one class only.
S Saturdays only.
X Except Sats., and School Holidays.
Z or *Z* Thursdays and Saturdays.
¶ "Halts" at Heath (High Level), between Cardiff and Llanishen; at Cefn On between Llanishen and Caerphilly; at Gilfach Fargoed, between Pengam (Glam.) and Bargoed.

1. Ystrad Mynach to Rhymney Bridge

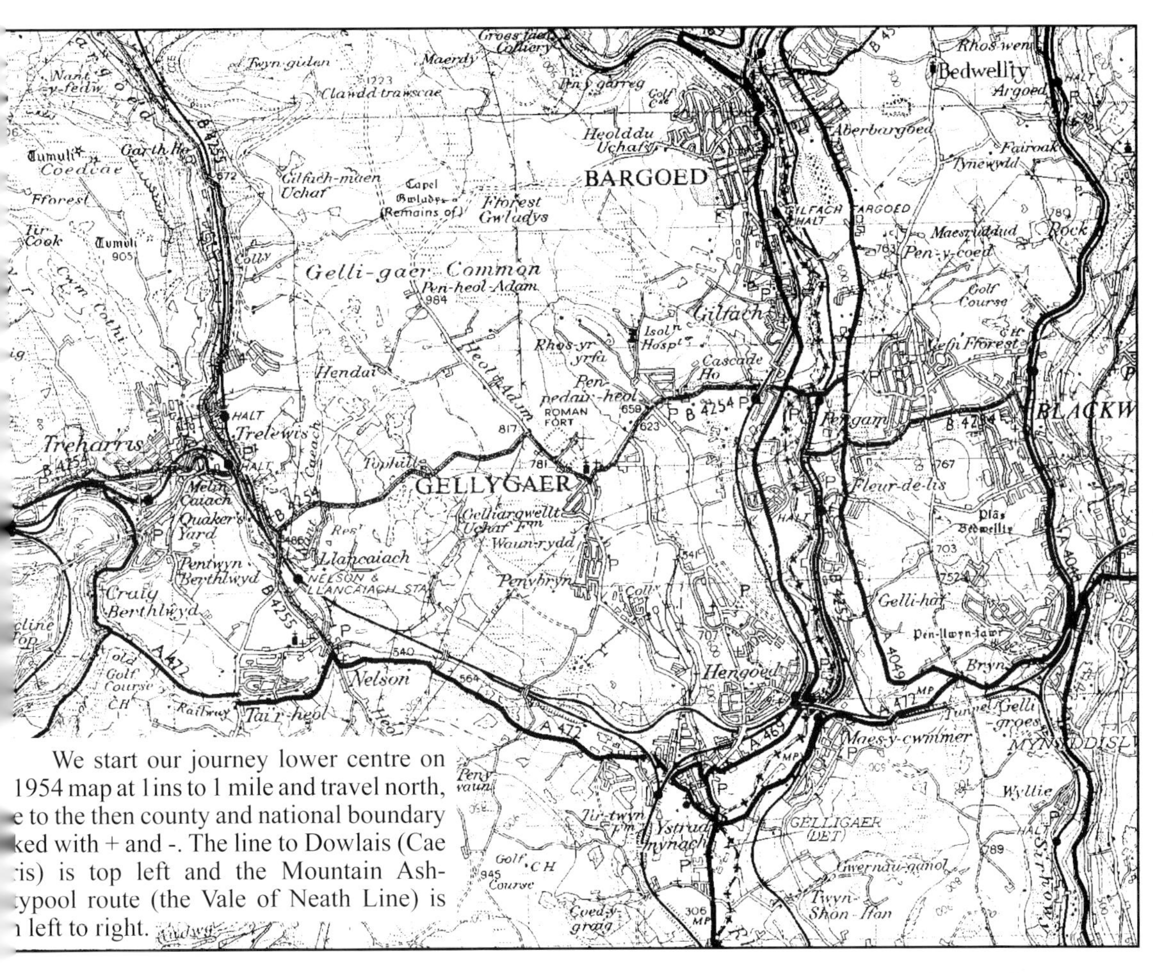

We start our journey lower centre on 1954 map at 1ins to 1 mile and travel north, e to the then county and national boundary ked with + and -. The line to Dowlais (Cae is) is top left and the Mountain Ash-ypool route (the Vale of Neath Line) is left to right.

SOUTH OF YSTRAD MYNACH

1. Passing South Box on 2nd June 1968 is a DMU bound for Cardiff. To the right of it is the down loop and on the left is the up refuge siding, later used by the engineers. (G.H.Tilt)

2. Photographed in July 1984 is South Box and its unusual structure for rods and wires. It was fitted with a 46-lever frame and was still in use in 2008, controlling the junction used by coal trains on the single line from Cwmbargoed. It was the only ex-RR box in use. (D.K.Jones coll.)

YSTRAD MYNACH

IV. The 1919 edition at 20ins to 1 mile has the station approach road between the diverging routes and also the single siding for local goods. Running north from North Junction is part of Cylla goods yard. North Box is above the word "Junction" and its 47-lever frame was in use until 19th September 1976. The lines on the right go to Hengoed; the upper ones to High Level and the lower ones to Low Level.

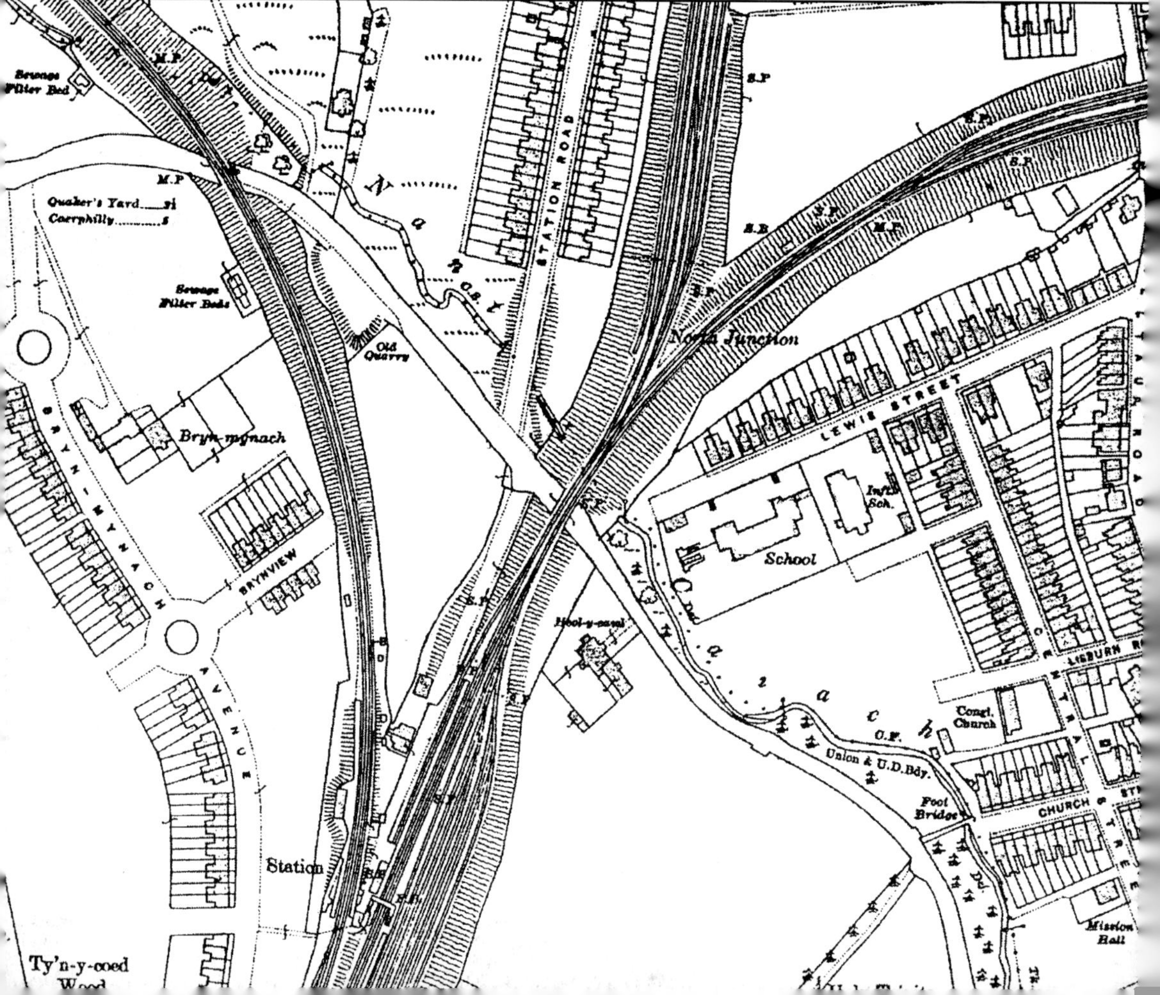

3. A down train approaches in about 1936 and the staggered platforms are evident. This configuration was used in several places by the RR, as it was generally safer before the advent of a footbridge. (Stations UK)

4. About to pass under the footbridge on 7th May 1957 is the 10.0am Cadoxton to Penallta Colliery empties. Hauling it is no. 5621, one of the 5600 class 0-6-2Ts introduced by the GWR in 1924. (S.Rickard/J&J coll.)

5. A northward panorama from the footbridge on 10th July 1958 includes part of the down yard, where wagons of coal could stand awaiting a ship. The goods yard seems full; it closed on 20th September 1965. (H.C.Casserley)

6. Passing through the site of the branch platforms on 26th March 1976 is no. 47378. They were last used in 1964. The coal train is running from Cwmbargoed to Aberthaw Power Station. (T.Heavyside)

7. Seen on the same day is the 11.14 Penarth to Rhymney and also the cottages built for the staff. The left signal is for the Cylla Branch. North Box is out of view; it closed a few months later, on 12th September. (T.Heavyside)

Other pictures of this station can be found in *Cardiff to Dowlais (Cae Harris)* in this series

Ystrad Mynach	1923	1929	1930	1933
Passenger tickets issued	91165	67718	60814	42059
Season tickets issued	294	730	802	742
Parcels forwarded	13510	14771	15476	18178
General goods forwarded (tons)	2793	3090	3505	3792
Coal and coke received (tons)	114	168	153	103
Other minerals received (tons)	11247	6900	7199	6834
General goods received (tons)	11325	15774	18409	13221
Trucks of livestock handled	246	311	334	260

8. Hauled by two class 37s, the train has its rear wagons on the Cylla Branch when photographed on 24th August 1983. As elsewhere, the goods yard had become a car park. (P.G.Barnes)

9. Sprinter no. 150282 worked the 09.47 from Penarth on 8th October 2008. It is about to return there at 10.28. One train per hour did so during that year. (N.W.Sprinks)

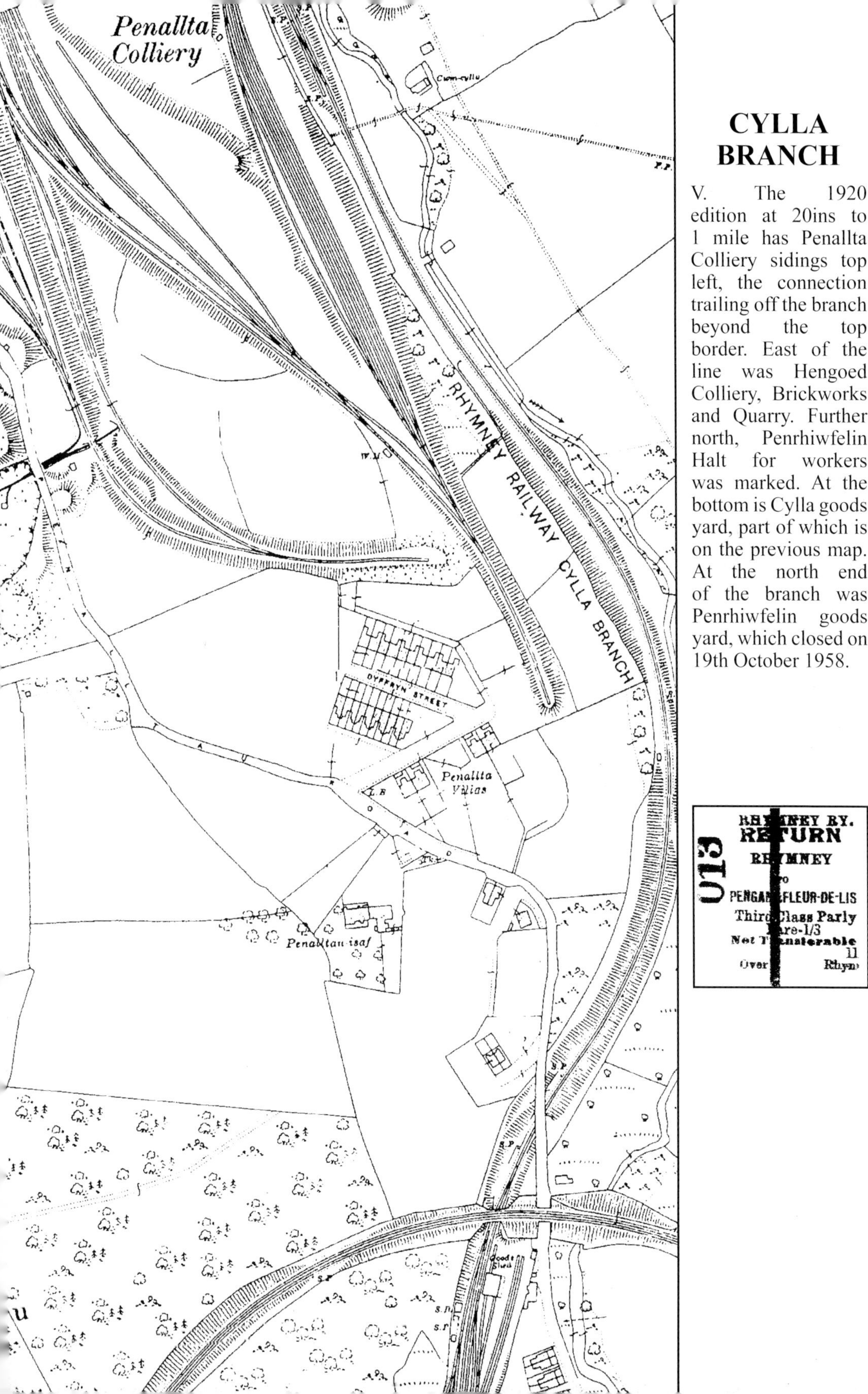

CYLLA BRANCH

V. The 1920 edition at 20ins to 1 mile has Penallta Colliery sidings top left, the connection trailing off the branch beyond the top border. East of the line was Hengoed Colliery, Brickworks and Quarry. Further north, Penrhiwfelin Halt for workers was marked. At the bottom is Cylla goods yard, part of which is on the previous map. At the north end of the branch was Penrhiwfelin goods yard, which closed on 19th October 1958.

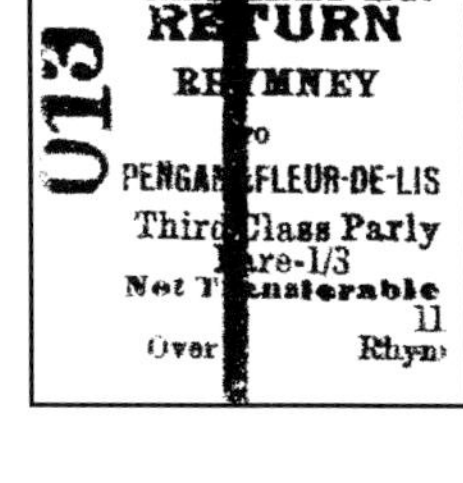

10. A northward view from a train bound for Rhymney on 28th August 1960 has Cylla goods shed and signal box in the distance, plus a gunpowder van on the right. This part of the branch opened on 1st August 1906 and the northern extremity followed in 1909. The box had 29 levers and functioned until 2nd September 1963. (M.Dart)

11. Running north out of the yard on 7th September 1957 is no. 6641, another 5600 class 0-6-2T. The upper signal is a RR somersault type and below it is a fixed distant. The bridge carries the Vale of Neath trains. (S.Rickard/J&J coll.)

12. There was a rare opportunity to photograph the northern box on 11th July 1959. This is Penrhiwfelin and its 27-lever frame was worked until 6th October 1971. Some ex-GWR locomotives were cut up here in 1959. (G.Adams/M.J.Stretton coll.)

13. The trailing junction to Penallta Colliery was photographed on 31st March 1972. Inside the colliery shed on that day was ex-GWR 0-6-0PT no. 7714, now on the Severn Valley. Coal production ceased in 1991. The first of two shafts was sunk in 1905 and production started in 1909. (M.Dart)

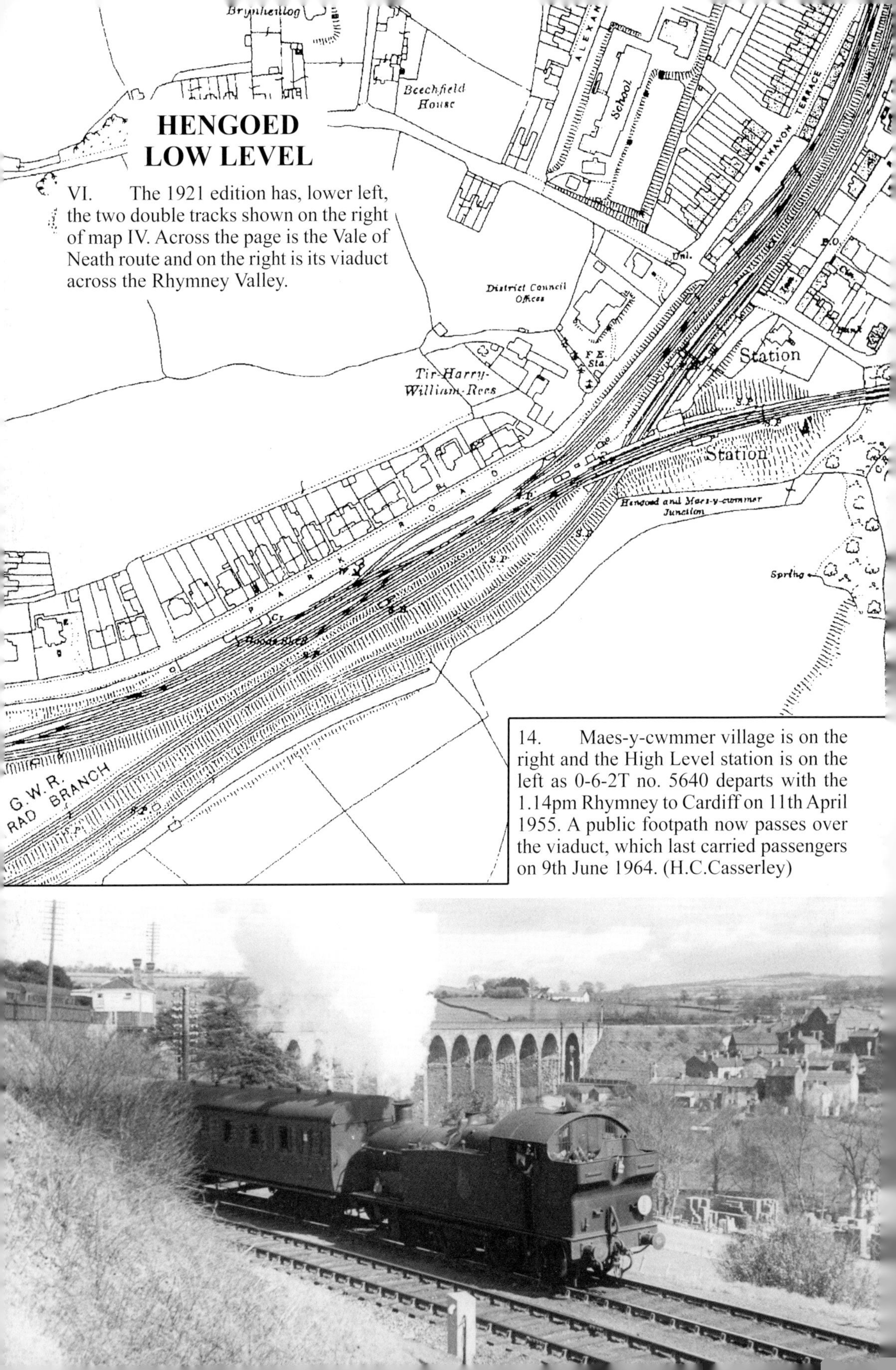

HENGOED LOW LEVEL

VI. The 1921 edition has, lower left, the two double tracks shown on the right of map IV. Across the page is the Vale of Neath route and on the right is its viaduct across the Rhymney Valley.

14. Maes-y-cwmmer village is on the right and the High Level station is on the left as 0-6-2T no. 5640 departs with the 1.14pm Rhymney to Cardiff on 11th April 1955. A public footpath now passes over the viaduct, which last carried passengers on 9th June 1964. (H.C.Casserley)

15. A southward view from the up platform at about the same time has the bridge and buildings of High Level beyond the footbridge. (H.C.Casserley)

16. The station is in the distance as no. 4101 leaves it with the 10.44 Rhymney to Cardiff on 23rd February 1956. The ground on the right had been occupied by the RR goods yard until 1st November 1925. (D.K.Jones coll.)

17. Looking west on 30th May 1964, we witness 0-6-2T no. 6684 rattling through with an empty coal train. Both exits and evidence of gas lighting are included. (J.C.Gillham)

High Level is illustrated in pictures 60 to 69 in our *Pontypool to Mountain Ash* album.

RHYMNEY RAILWAY
CARDIFF To
RHYMNEY
THIRD CLASS PARLY
2910
Over 108 Rhymney Revised Fare 3/3

Gt Western Ry Gt Western Ry
Cardiff Parade Cardiff Parade
TO
RHYMNEY
via Llanishen&Brithdir
THIRD CLASS
2/10 Fare 2/10
Issued subject to the conditions & regulations set out in the Company's Time Tables Bills & Notices
Rhymney Rhymney
2401 2401

18. A panorama from the High Level station on the same day reveals that the RR station was built with doors on both levels. The road in the foreground served both stations and there was a common booking office by that time. (J.C.Gillham)

19. Our final view from the survey of that day is from the east and features the hipped roof of the High Level building. The station had been "Rhymney Junction" until 1906, when "Hengoed & Maesycwmmer" was used. The distinction of "Levels" was applied from July 1924. (J.C.Gillham)

20. The Vale of Neath route closed to passengers and goods on the same day in 1964 and only the bridge abutments were visible on 26th March 1976 as the 13.14 Penarth to Rhymney pulled in. A new bridge has been provided over the line on these abutments, carrying a footpath and cycleway. (T.Heavyside)

21. Turning round, we see the same train standing under the original footbridge, the only structure remaining from the past. Out of view is the site of the 36-lever signal box, which lasted until 24th January 1966. (T.Heavyside)

22. This is the scene on 8th August 2003. The curve between the VofN and RR routes had been closed on 6th May 1963. It had been used by excursions and workmens services. (P.Jones)

PENGAM (GLAM.)

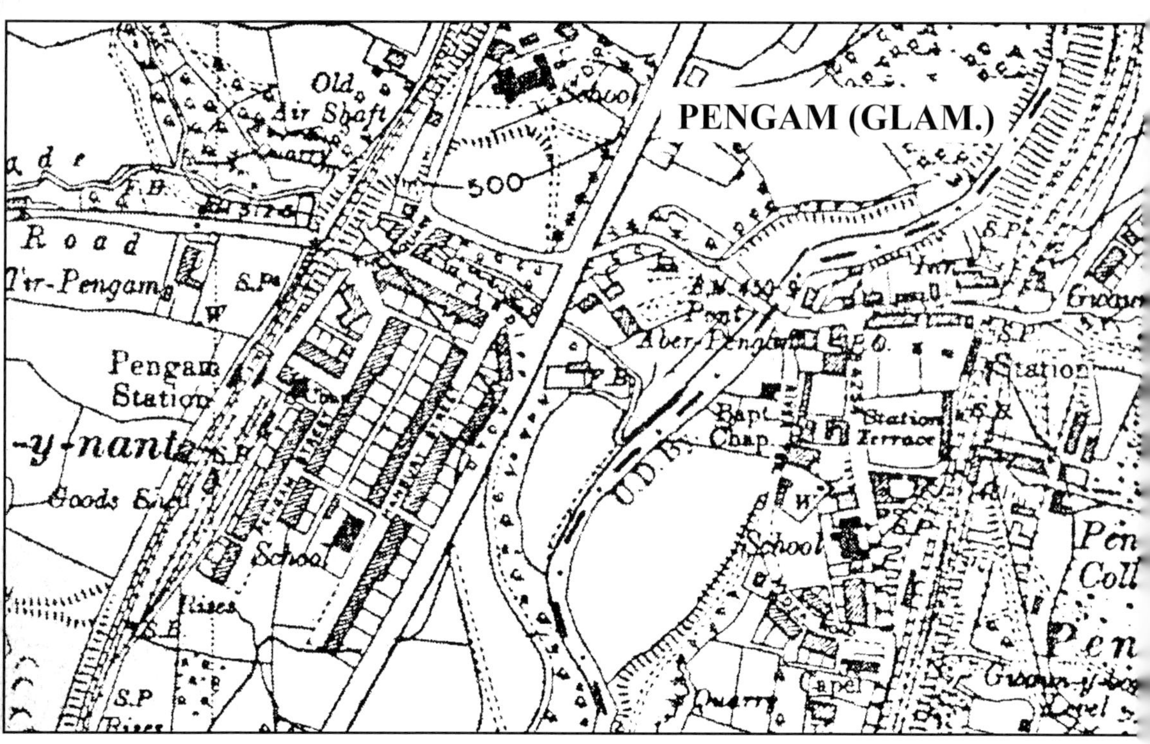

VII. The 1938 edition enlarged to 12ins to 1 mile shows both Pengam stations, Glamorgan being to the left of the dots and dashes of the county boundary in the river. South of the station is the signal box (S.B.), which had 21 levers and worked until 5th April 1965.

23. The main buildings were on the down side, which was the side of most residential development. There was a passenger staff of 14 in 1930, which was reduced to 12 by 1936. The goods department listed 31 and 26 in those years, these figures including those working on coal traffic. (R.M.Casserley coll.)

24. The station is in the background as freight from Cardiff Docks to Bargoed passes on 27th April 1957. No. 38 was an ex-RR 0-6-2T. (S.Rickard/J&J coll.)

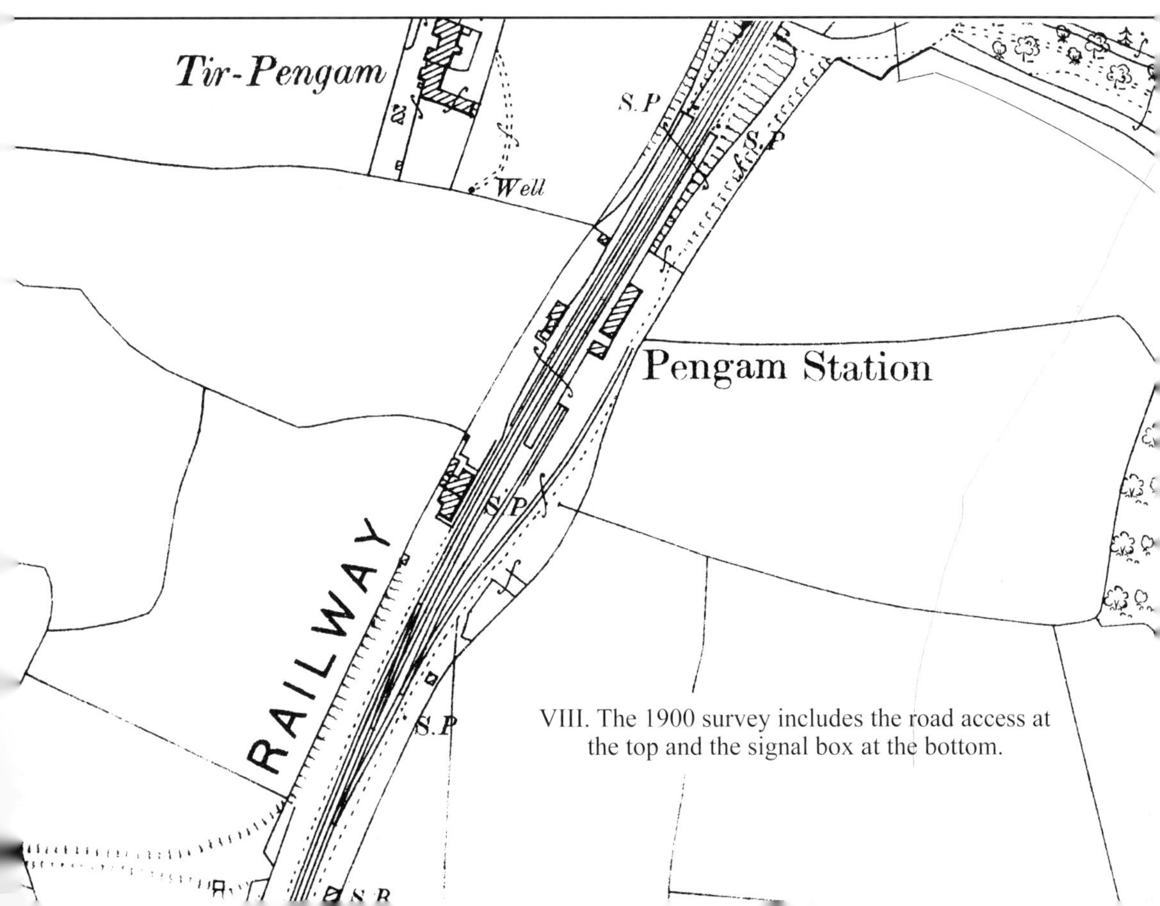

VIII. The 1900 survey includes the road access at the top and the signal box at the bottom.

25. The name was plain "Pengam" initially, and "Pengam & Fleur-de-Lis" from 1st February 1909 until 1st July 1924. It was as shown from then until 6th May 1968, when (Glam.) was dropped. The photograph is from 1958. (Stations UK)

26. We look south on 2nd June 1968 and see the site of the goods yard, which closed on 28th September 1964. It had a 6-ton crane. The canopy was rebuilt as shown. The goods yard became part of a police station compound. (G.H.Tilt)

27. No. 37414 hauled the four coaches of the 16.50 extra from Cardiff Central to Rhymney on 18th March 2000. Owing to a shortage of DMUs, some peak time trains were loco-hauled for around ten years. (D.H.Mitchell)

28. Standard brick-built shelters arrived at many stations in the late 1970s. "Pacers" began to appear in 1992 and no. 142076 is departing for Bargoed on 14th August 2008. (H.Ballantyne)

NORTH OF PENGAM

29. Bargoed Pits Junction is lower left on the map opposite and was recorded on 28th August 1960 as 0-6-2T no. 5603 waits on the branch. The 32-lever signal box is lower left on the next map; it was in use until 4th October 1976 and was replaced by a ground frame. The line into the pits was opened in 1904 and was closed on 23rd May 1982. The other aspect of this box can be seen in picture 92. (M.Dart/Transport Treasury)

Pengam (Glam.)	1923	1929	1930	1933
Passenger tickets issued	139116	76993	71958	59119
Season tickets issued	274	592	540	533
Parcels forwarded	16632	18093	21929	32575
General goods forwarded (tons)	307	6297	5593	4248
Coal and coke received (tons)	451	1180	1303	384
Other minerals received (tons)	12729	12879	10643	5332
General goods received (tons)	3651	43063	45607	32030
Trucks of livestock handled	2	81	40	2

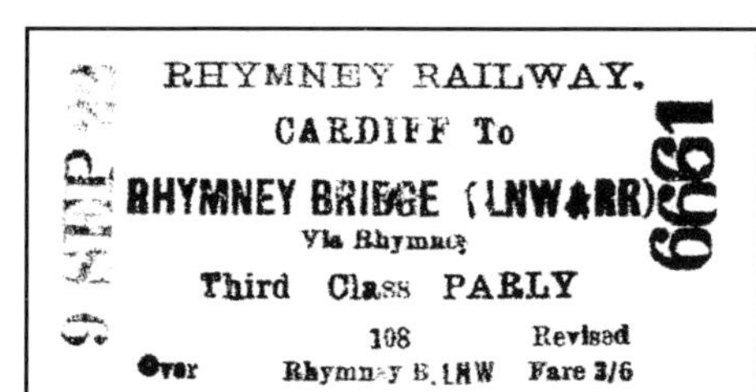

GILFACH FARGOED

IX. The 1920 extract at 12ins to 1 mile has the RR on the left and the B&MR on the right. This diverges at Aberbargoed Junction; the line to the right ran to New Tredegar until 31st December 1962, when the Brecon to Newport passenger service was also withdrawn. These trains ran from top left to lower right and passed over the Bargoed Pits tracks, which ran in the tunnel shown. A single line to Britannia Colliery (lower right) remained until January 1977. Coal was subsequently worked via Bargoed Colliery until May 1982. Gilfach signal box, marked near the pit, had a 21-lever frame, which was used from 1892 until 1932.

30. The halt opened on 1st April 1908 and is seen from the south on 2nd June 1968. It is top left on the map, close to the ex-B&MR connection between the two routes in the valley. This line rises to the right of the signal. Far right are the cooling towers. (G.H.Tilt)

31. The platforms were refaced in the 1950s, but not lengthened. This is the situation in 1984, after substantial track upgrades; we look south. (D.K.Jones coll.)

32. A northward panorama in October 2008 reveals little change, except evidence of highway improvement following spoil heap removal. All the other platforms on the route were lengthened in 2008 to accommodate six cars, but only one per hour stopped here. (N.W.Sprinks)

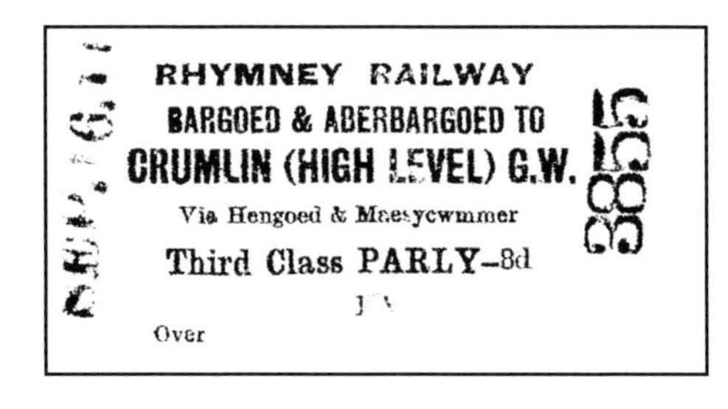

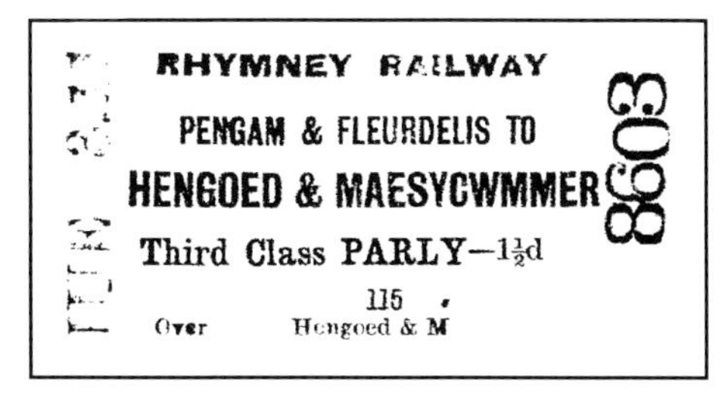

SOUTH OF BARGOED

33. A southward panorama from the end of the platform on 9th May 1953 features 0-6-2T no. 5635 silhouetted against the grim man-made scenery. Most tips eventually became green or were removed; these have gone. (S.Rickard/J&J coll.)

BRITISH RLYS(W) BRITISH RLYS(W)
HALF DAY EXCURSION RETURN
Brithdir Brithdir
TO
NINIAN PARK
PLATFORM
AND BACK
via YstradM&Penrhos or Llanishen
HIRD CLASS
NinianPark Ninian Park
FOR CONDITIONS SEE BACK W.D
3672 3672

RHYMNEY RAILWAY.
PONTLOTTYN To
RHYMNEY BRIDGE (L&NW&RR)
Third Class PARLY—2½d.
117
Over] RhymneyB'dge
2018

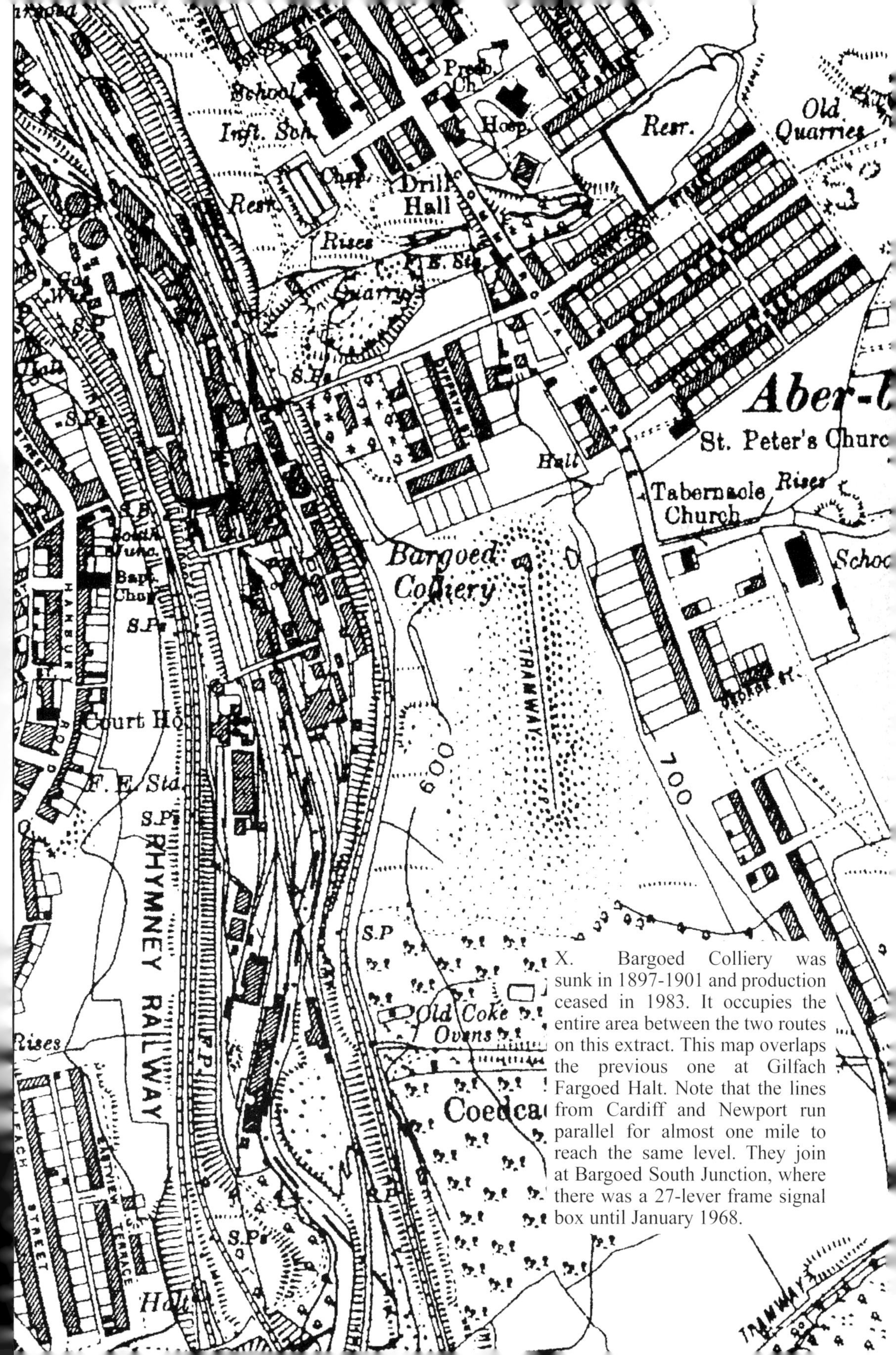

X. Bargoed Colliery was sunk in 1897-1901 and production ceased in 1983. It occupies the entire area between the two routes on this extract. This map overlaps the previous one at Gilfach Fargoed Halt. Note that the lines from Cardiff and Newport run parallel for almost one mile to reach the same level. They join at Bargoed South Junction, where there was a 27-lever frame signal box until January 1968.

34. Tips were still evident as the 16.28 Rhymney to Cardiff Bute Road passed the decaying remains of Bargoed Colliery on 29th June 1981. It closed in 1977. The train is running on the single line, the other then being along through siding. (T.Heavyside)

35. The 14.16 from Bargoed to Cardiff on 13th March 2000 was an additional working to take crowds to an event in the Millenium Stadium. Leading is no. 47475 and trailing is no. 47781. There is evidence of tip clearance. (D.H.Mitchell)

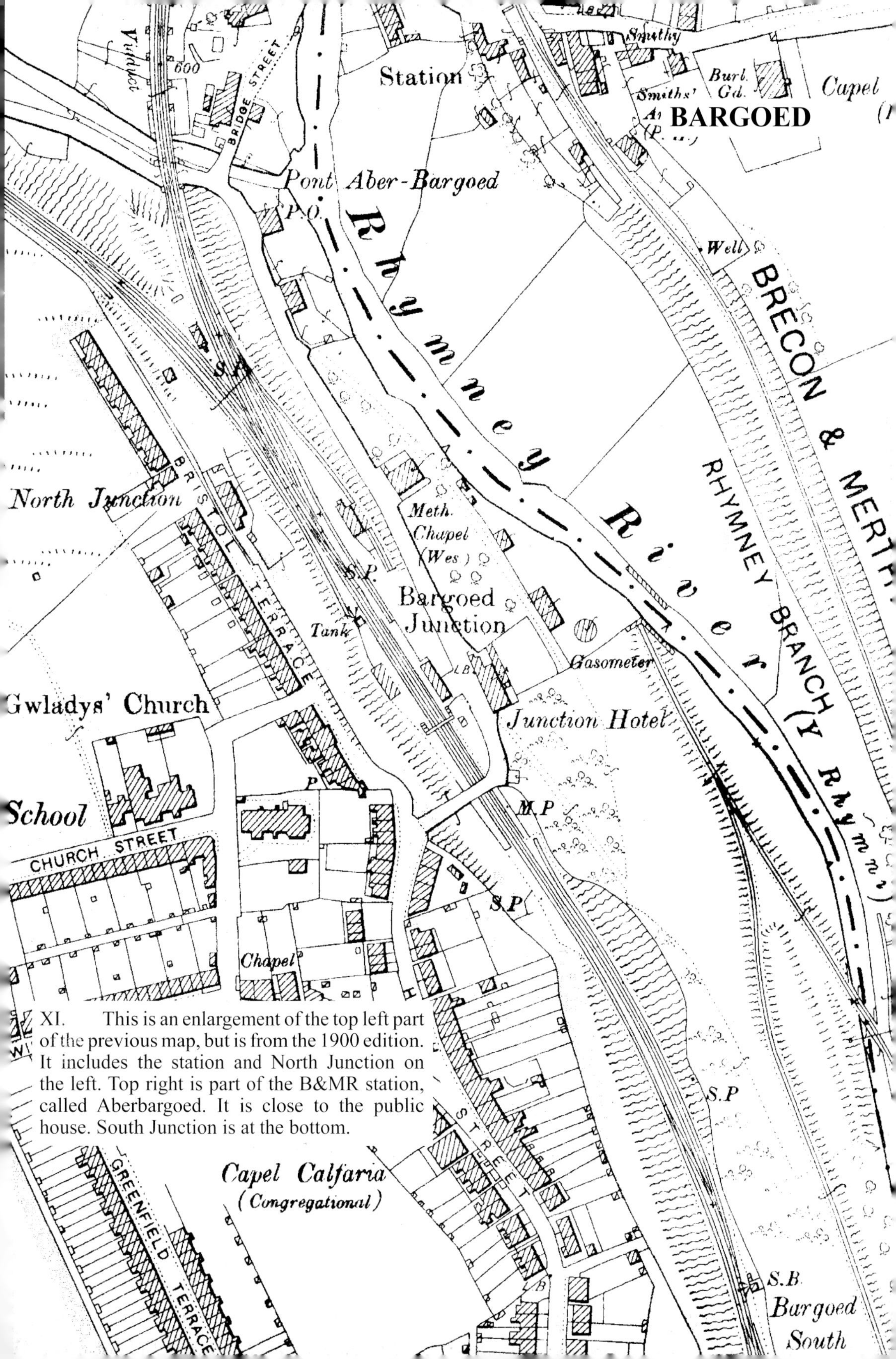

XI. This is an enlargement of the top left part of the previous map, but is from the 1900 edition. It includes the station and North Junction on the left. Top right is part of the B&MR station, called Aberbargoed. It is close to the public house. South Junction is at the bottom.

36. There were 36 men here in 1923, but only 18 by 1933. An up train leaves for Deri behind no. 9616 on 2nd May 1959. The station suffix was "& Aber Bargoed" from 1st June 1905 until 1st July 1924. (S.Rickard/J&J coll.)

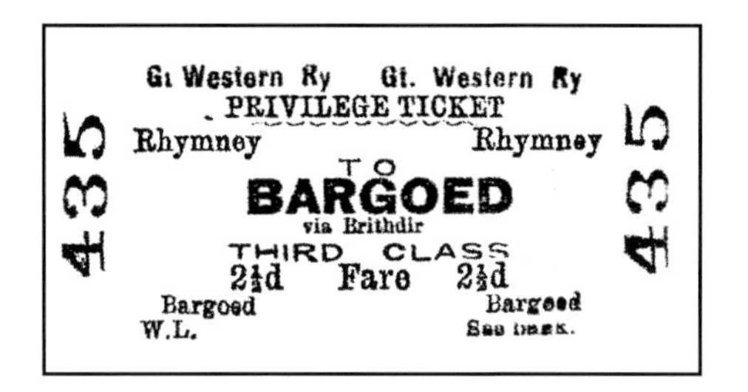

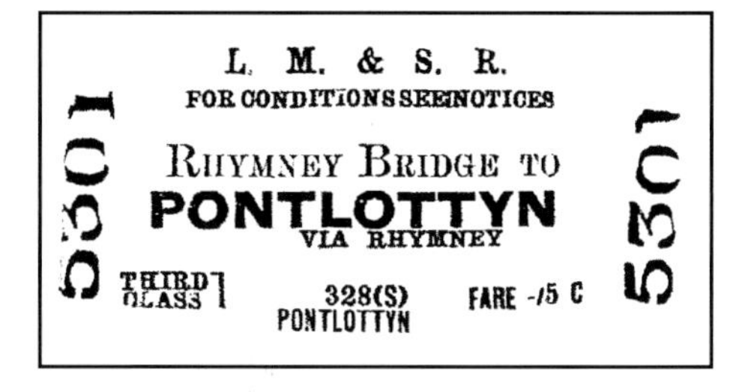

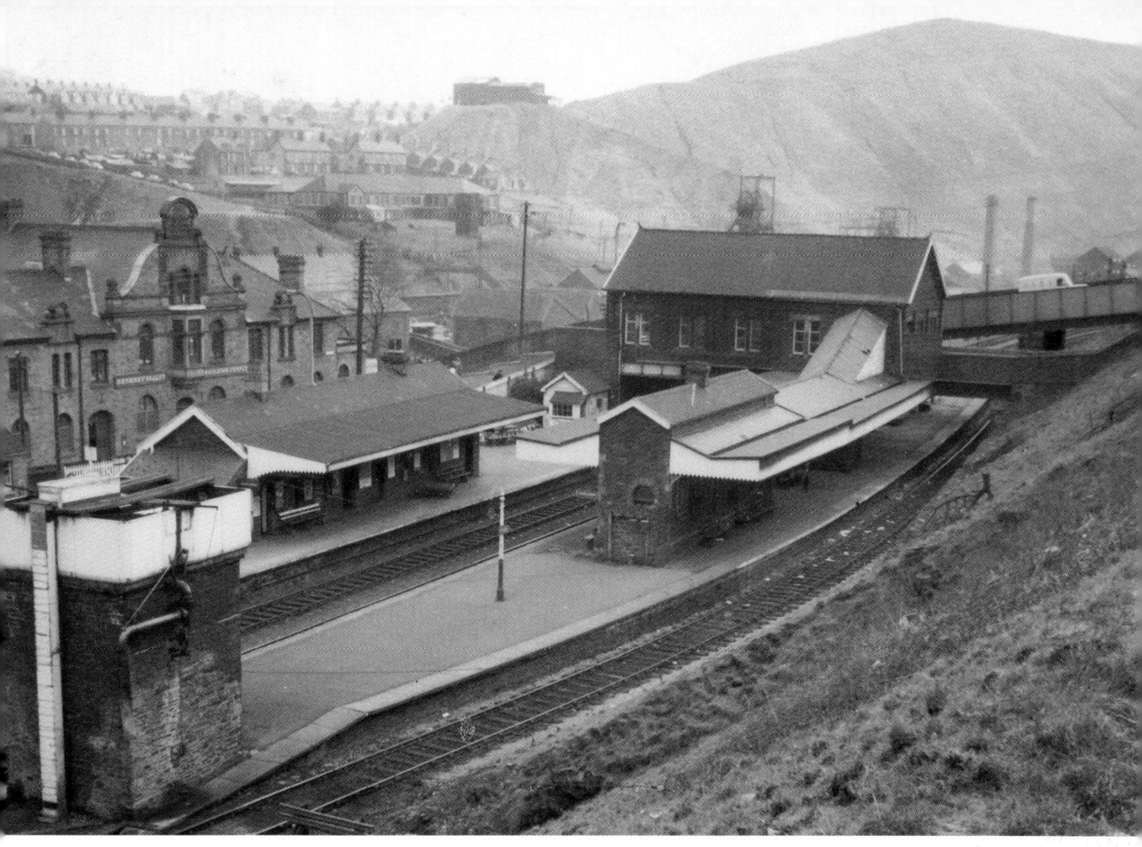

37. A fine overall southward view from April 1965 has a familiar background. The nearest through track was added in 1900, converting the up platform into an island. Note that the elevated ticket office has a footbridge to it. This shows on the map. (B.W.L.Brooksbank)

38. On 9th November 1970, major alterations were brought into use, controlled by the new central signal box. A facing crossover south of the station permitted up trains to use the former down platform, the up one being taken out of use. North of Bargoed, the former up line became the bidirectional single line to Rhymney; the former down line becoming the McLaren Dump line. On closure of the latter in 1976, a short length was retained at the Bargoed end as a turnback siding for terminating trains. The branch northwest to Ogilvie Colliery was singled in November 1970. (D.K.Jones coll.)

39. North Box (44 levers) had been in the V of the junction, as shown in picture 36, but it was replaced by this flat-roofed model, with 51 levers, on 9th November 1970. It is seen on 25th September 1980, while the 13.05 Penarth to Rhymney unusually uses the goods line. The Ogilvie branch had remained open for coal until 3rd September 1978. The box and frame had come from Cymmer Afan. (D.H.Mitchell)

Other views of this station can be found in our *Brecon to Newport* album in pictures 77-82. The 1920 map is therein.

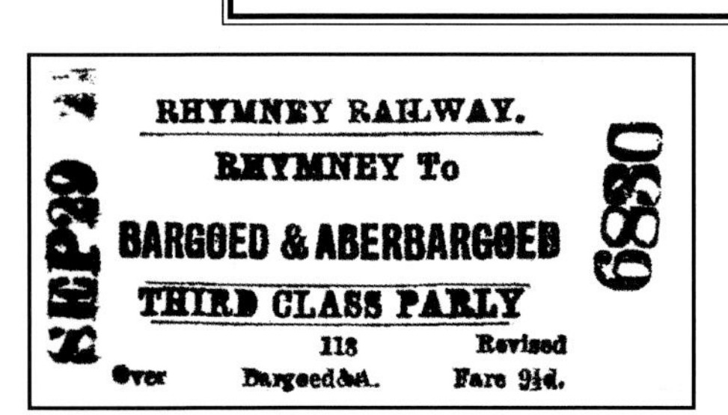

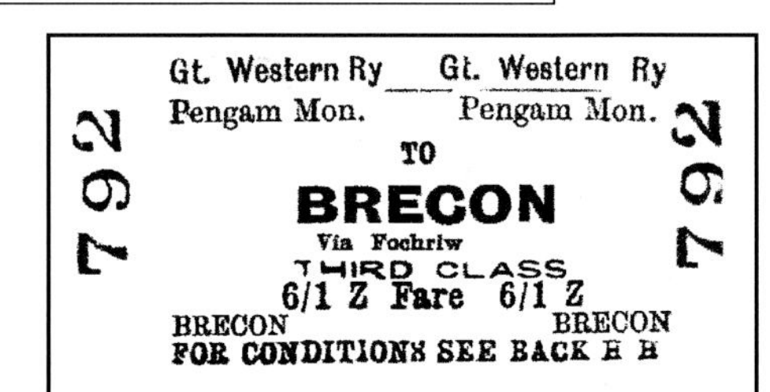

40. The eaves of the goods shed can be seen, as the driver of no. 152040 surrenders the single line token to the signalman on 8th October 2008. The spur on the left was laid on 20th November 2005 on the alignment seen in picture 36 and was an emergency run-off. Its provision allowed frequency from the south to be doubled to four per hour. (N.W.Sprinks)

41. The up platform was reinstated in July 2001 and a footbridge with lifts was provided. The old road bridge was replaced with this tunnel which carries the new bypass. No. 143602 worked the 13.47 from Penarth on 12the February 2009 and was usually terminating at the new up platform. This was due to a late running train from Rhymney.The old building survived, although devoid of chimney pots. (V.Mitchell)

NORTH OF BARGOED

XII. The 1954 edition at 1ins to 1 mile includes the remainder of both routes, Bargoed being at the bottom, right of centre. Tredegar is featured in our *Sirhowy Valley Line* album and Ebbw Vale is in *Abertillery and Ebbw Vale Lines*.

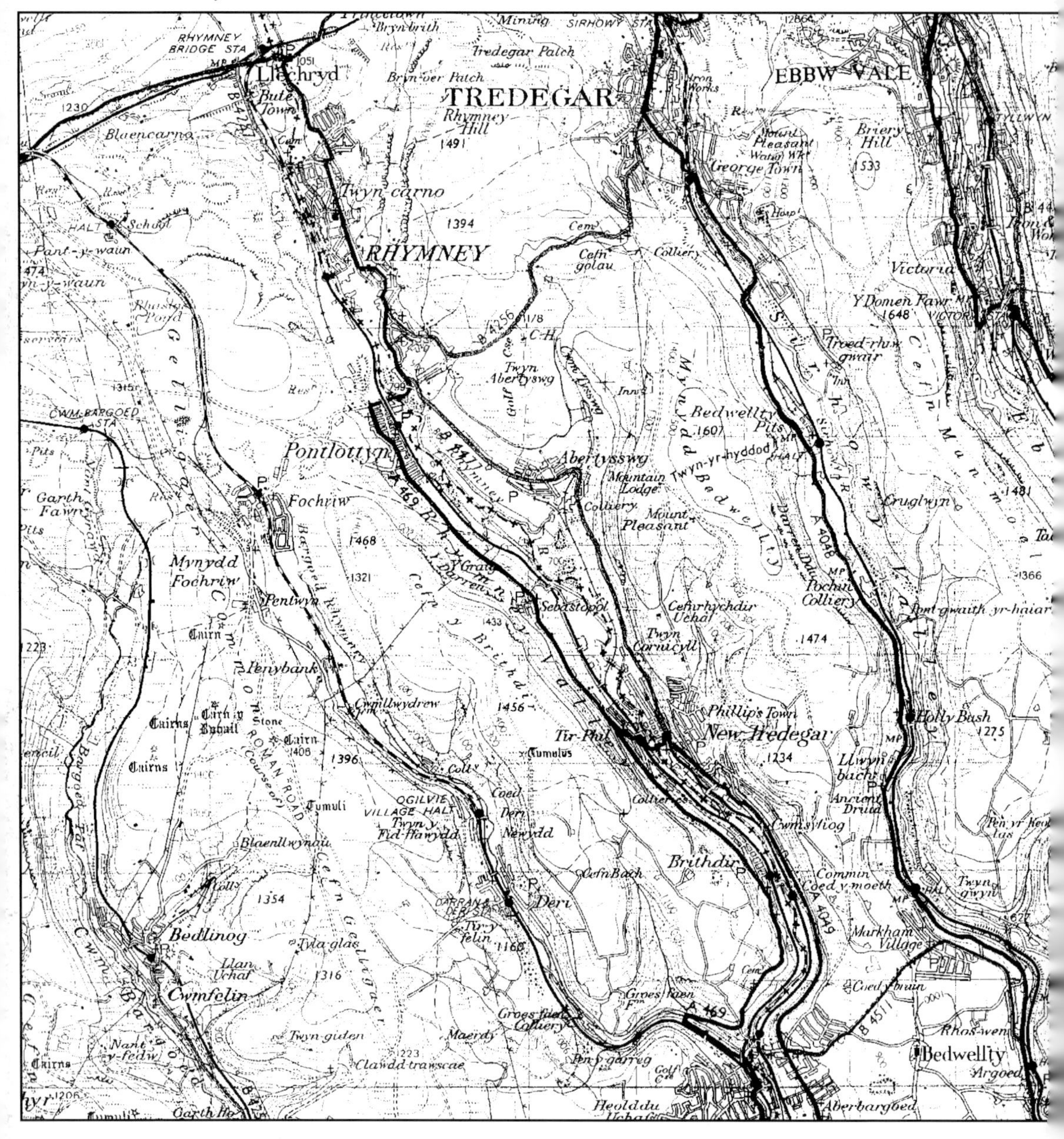

42. Bargoed Viaduct is seen from a train bound for Deri on 12th July 1956. North Box faces the lines leading to the goods yard, which closed on 22nd March 1963. (H.C.Casserley)

43. It is 29th June 1981 and part of the signal box can be seen above the rear car of the train, which is travelling to the left, bound for Rhymney. (T.Heavyside)

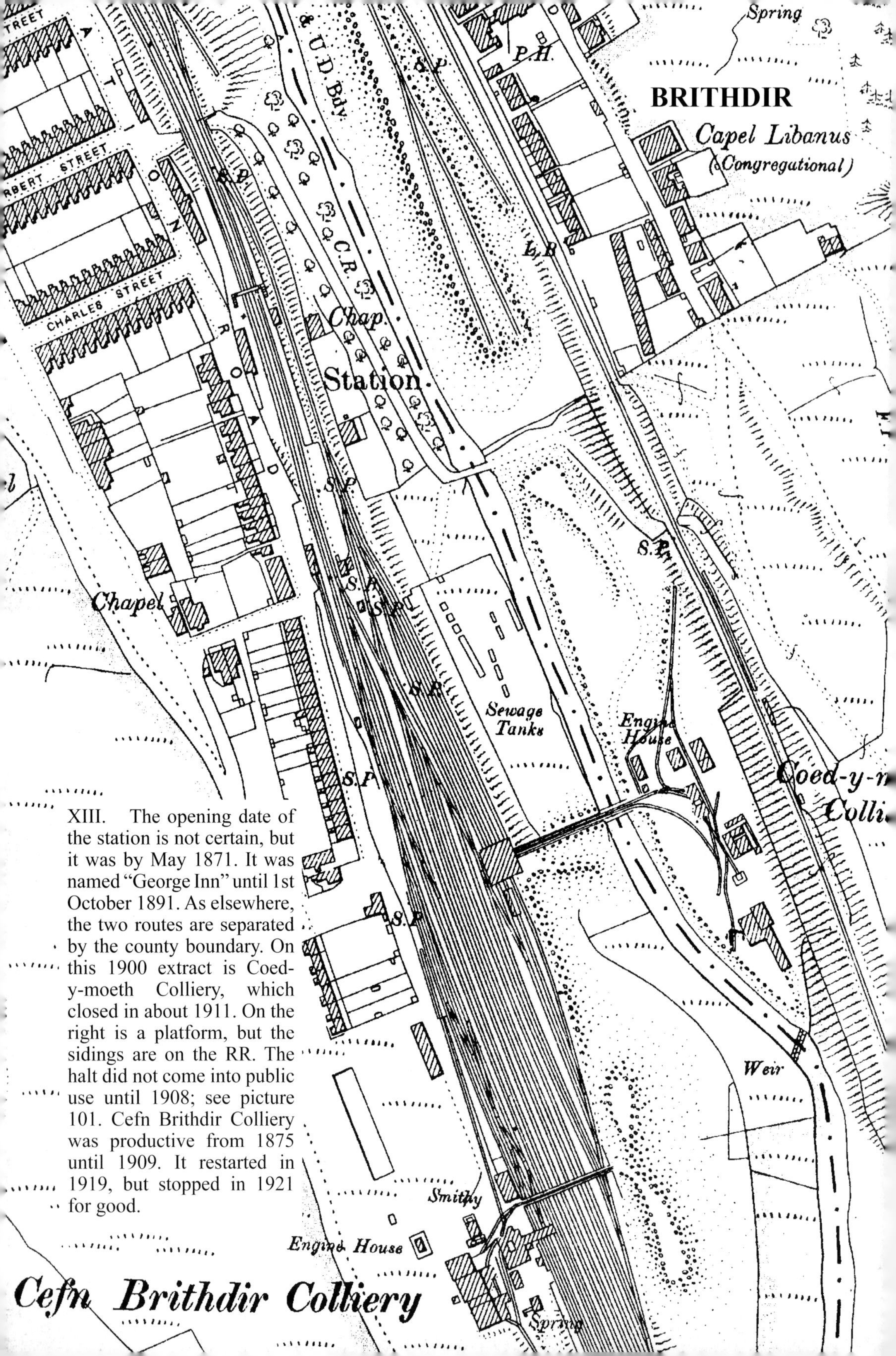

XIII. The opening date of the station is not certain, but it was by May 1871. It was named "George Inn" until 1st October 1891. As elsewhere, the two routes are separated by the county boundary. On this 1900 extract is Coed-y-moeth Colliery, which closed in about 1911. On the right is a platform, but the sidings are on the RR. The halt did not come into public use until 1908; see picture 101. Cefn Brithdir Colliery was productive from 1875 until 1909. It restarted in 1919, but stopped in 1921 for good.

44. There was a staff of seven or eight in the 1930s. This 1958 westward panorama is from the top right corner of the map and emphasises the bleak surroundings, complete with waste tips close to the houses. (Stations UK)

45. A view north in April 1965 has a trackbed on the right, which carried a line north to Elliot Colliery from about 1890. (B.W.L.Brooksbank)

46. A train from Rhymney arrives on 3rd July 1966 and our view from the footbridge includes a remnant of the B&MR behind it. (G.H.Tilt)

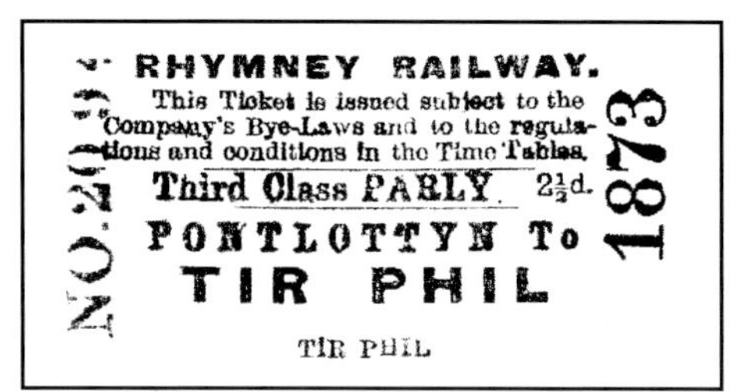
RHYMNEY RAILWAY.
This Ticket is issued subject to the Company's Bye-Laws and to the regulations and conditions in the Time Tables.
Third Class PARLY. 2½d.
PONTLOTTYN To
TIR PHIL
TIR PHIL
NO.20
1873

Brithdir	1923	1929	1930	1933
Passenger tickets issued	102502	45992	49143	47515
Season tickets issued	55	64	66	62
Parcels forwarded	2862	2623	2713	4020
General goods forwarded (tons)	250	138	237	166
Coal and coke received (tons)	7	24	16	38
Other minerals received (tons)	2152	1443	1361	1432
General goods received (tons)	2605	14229	12636	5487
Trucks of livestock handled	-	-	-	-

47. Looking in the other direction two years later, we glimpse the colliery sidings and down goods loop. Their official closure was February 1969. The 38-lever signal box in the distance had closed the following month. There had been a public siding on the right until April 1957. (G.H.Tilt)

48. In the foreground is part of the 2008 platform extension. The down platform had been disused since 1970; the route had been doubled in 1892. (N.W.Sprinks)

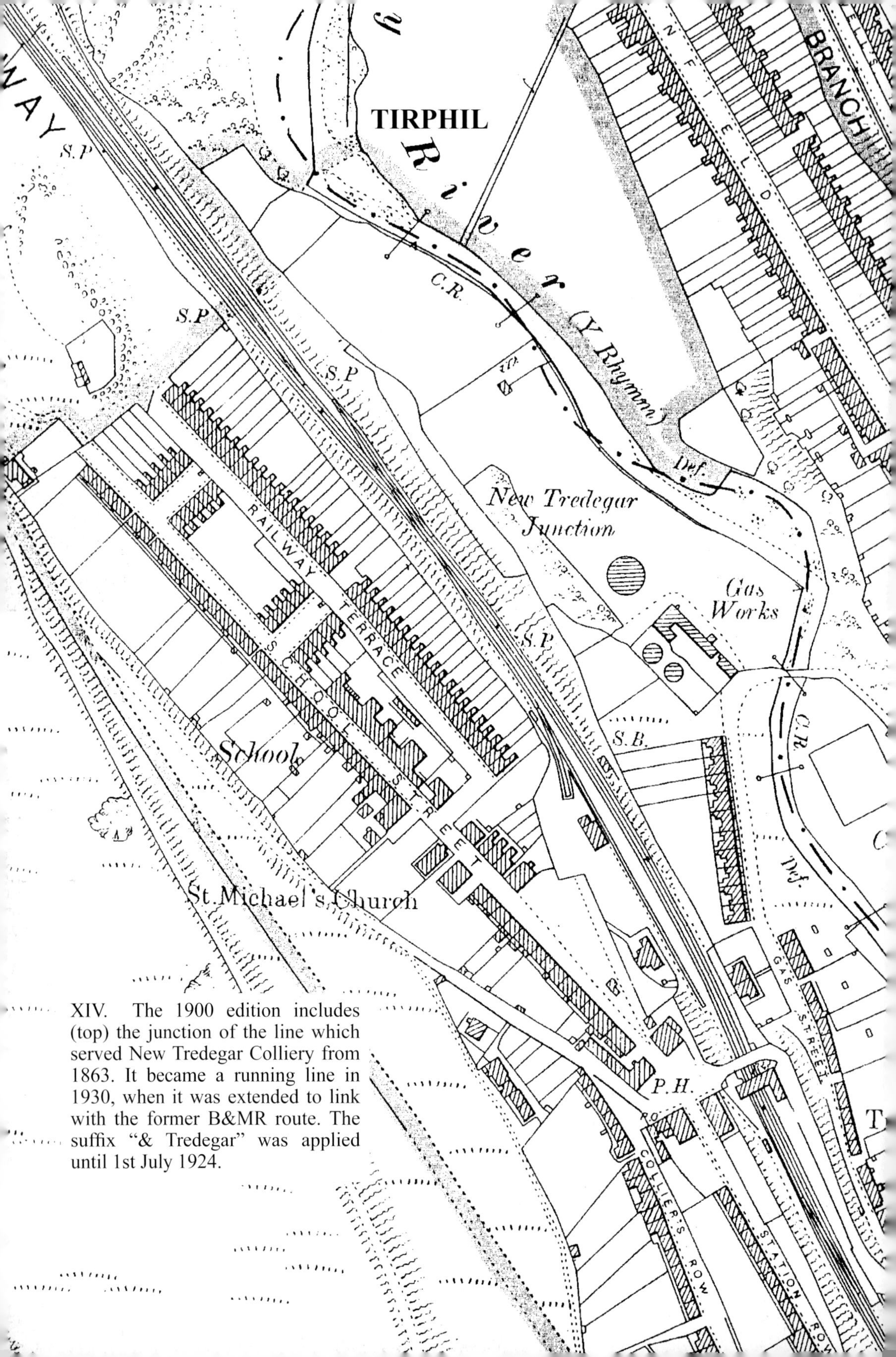

XIV. The 1900 edition includes (top) the junction of the line which served New Tredegar Colliery from 1863. It became a running line in 1930, when it was extended to link with the former B&MR route. The suffix "& Tredegar" was applied until 1st July 1924.

49. The staff numbered 12 for most of the 1930s; selected employees posed earlier for a postcard producer. The high level building probably dates from the doubling of 1892. (LGRP)

50. A 1958 southward panorama features the footbridge which replaced the building across the track. The six-car train had coaches beyond the platform end. (Stations UK)

51. Another 1958 record features the 32-lever signal box, which closed with the singling in 1970. However, two parallel tracks remained in use from Bargoed until 1976, the eastern one curving away here to serve McLaren's Dump via the 1930 line across the valley. (Stations UK)

Tirphil	1923	1929	1930	1933
Passenger tickets issued	132408	84907	86982	92763
Season tickets issued	231	571	515	388
Parcels forwarded	19581	17256	16101	16210
General goods forwarded (tons)	236	420	1719	213
Coal and coke received (tons)	10	242	242	261
Other minerals received (tons)	3247	2191	1477	383
General goods received (tons)	2945	11673	7827	2812
Trucks of livestock handled	8	3	3	-

52. The siding north of the station originally served a coal level, but it became part of the small goods yard until its closure on 4th January 1965. A crane of 2-ton capacity was provided and it was still in place, along with the goods shed, in 2008. (G.H.Tilt)

53. None of the earlier structures remained to be photographed in 2008, but at least the platform had been lengthened recently to take six cars. (N.W.Sprinks)

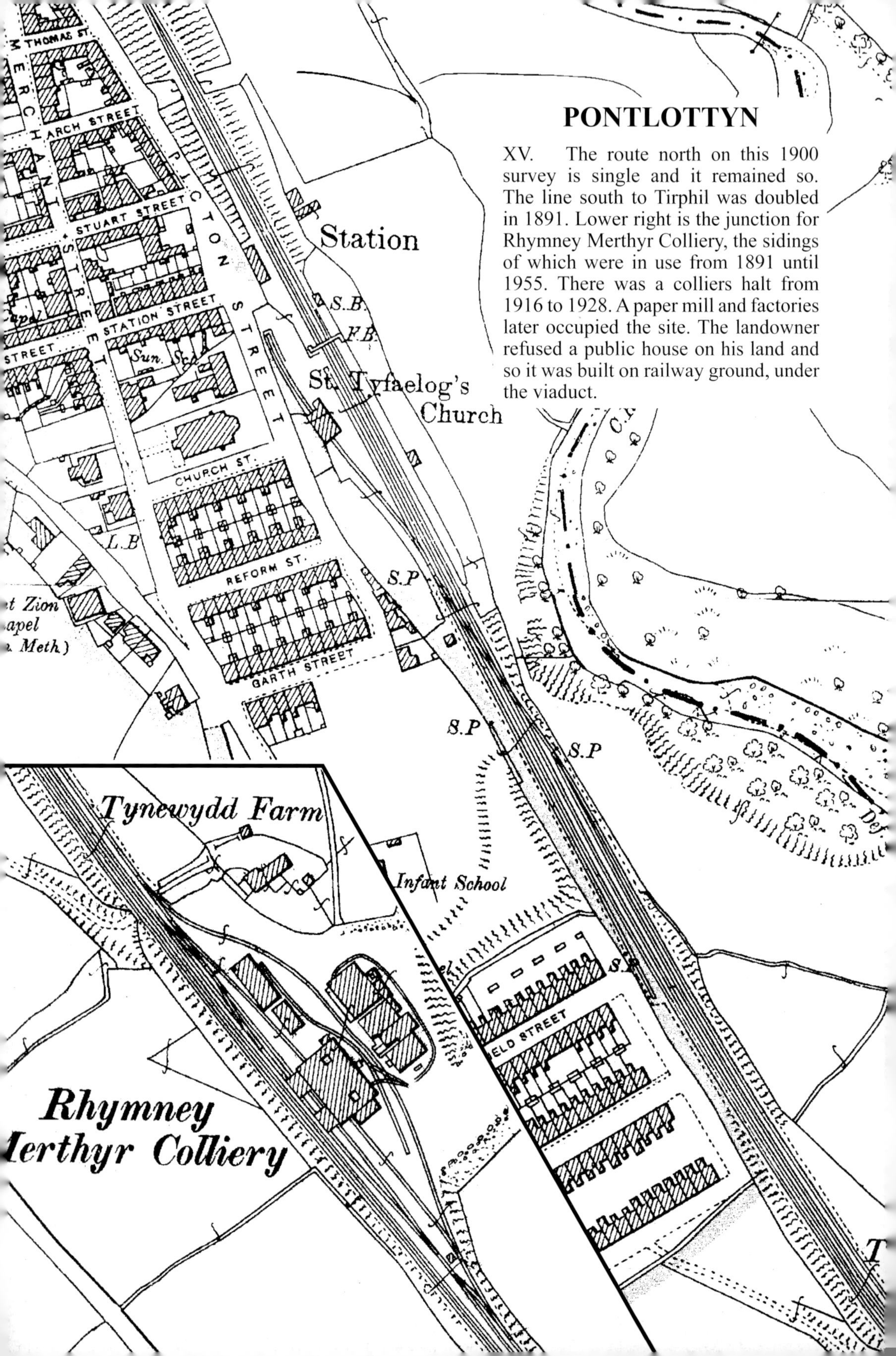

PONTLOTTYN

XV. The route north on this 1900 survey is single and it remained so. The line south to Tirphil was doubled in 1891. Lower right is the junction for Rhymney Merthyr Colliery, the sidings of which were in use from 1891 until 1955. There was a colliers halt from 1916 to 1928. A paper mill and factories later occupied the site. The landowner refused a public house on his land and so it was built on railway ground, under the viaduct.

54. The station opened in November 1862 and a large goods shed followed later. Its roof is in the background. The signal box (left) had 18 levers and served from 1890 until 1970. (Lens of Sutton coll.)

Pontlottyn	1923	1929	1930	1933
Passenger tickets issued	104024	70108	88108	76575
Season tickets issued	332	418	442	295
Parcels forwarded	12479	10059	12017	13212
General goods forwarded (tons)	248	165	141	57
Coal and coke received (tons)	246	91	53	73
Other minerals received (tons)	1912	293	225	234
General goods received (tons)	1517	603	691	690
Trucks of livestock handled	3	1	3	-

55. There were around a dozen employees in the early 1930s. Another of the RR's staggered platform arrangement survived until the singling of 1970. The viaduct parapet is in the distance. (Stations UK)

56. On the right of this 1967 southward view is part of the goods yard, which was in use until 27th November 1967. On the left is the lamp room and the "cow horn" for catching the single line tablet hoop. (J.C.Gillham)

57. Two chapels are evident as the 08.52 Barry Island to Rhymney runs up the valley on 25th September 1980. Much light paint has brightened the once dreary landscape. (D.H.Mitchell)

58. No. 50031 heads the 14.38 Merthyr to Rhymney special on 9th August 1998. The platform is just beyond the 129yd long Pontlottyn Viaduct, but only its lamp posts are visible. (D.H.Mitchell)

59. On Saturday 11th October 2008, the two "Sprinters" working the 12.29 from Rhymney were running to Barry Island, instead of Penarth, due to engineering work. (N.W.Sprinks)

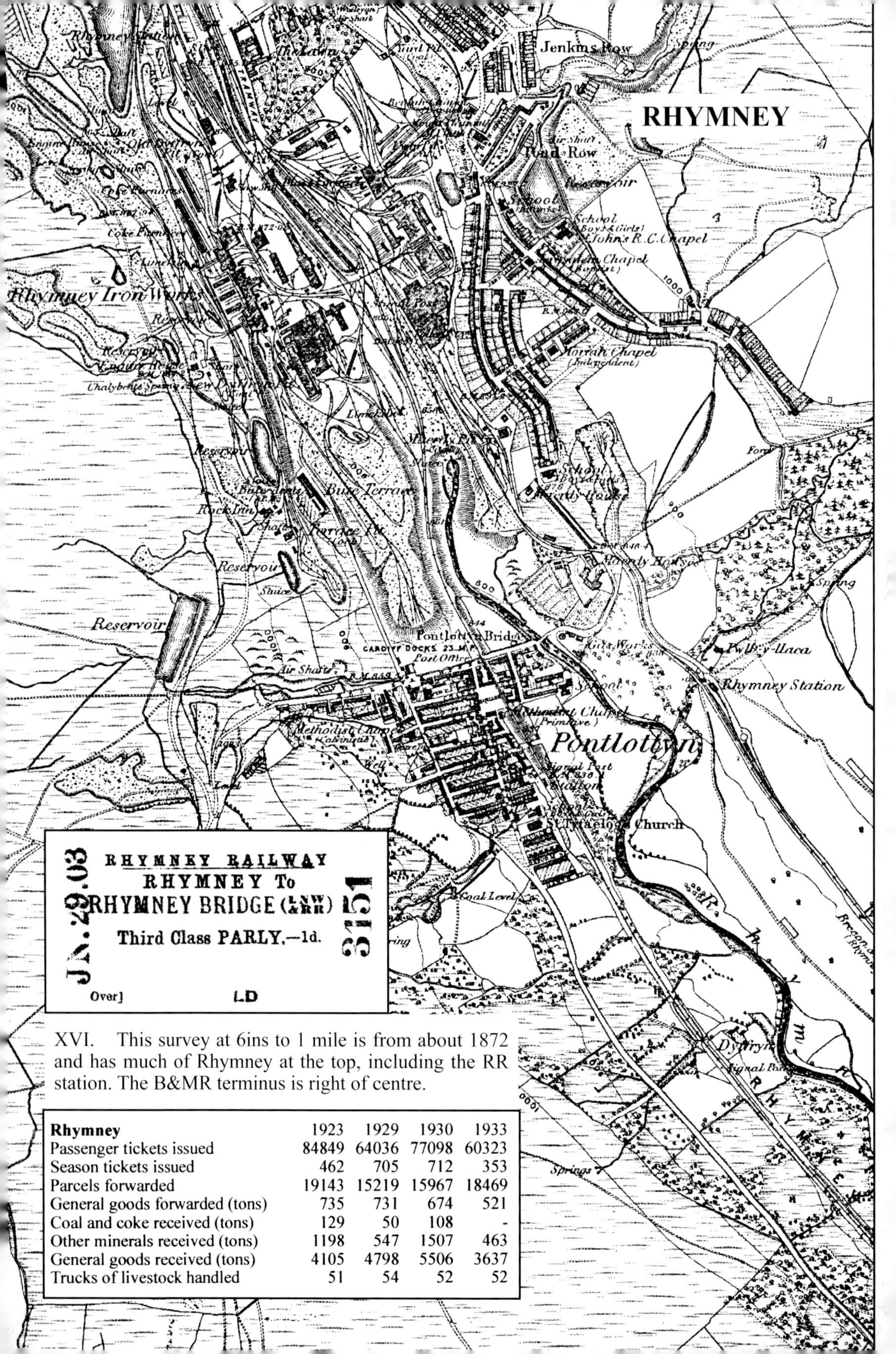

XVI. This survey at 6ins to 1 mile is from about 1872 and has much of Rhymney at the top, including the RR station. The B&MR terminus is right of centre.

Rhymney	1923	1929	1930	1933
Passenger tickets issued	84849	64036	77098	60323
Season tickets issued	462	705	712	353
Parcels forwarded	19143	15219	15967	18469
General goods forwarded (tons)	735	731	674	521
Coal and coke received (tons)	129	50	108	-
Other minerals received (tons)	1198	547	1507	463
General goods received (tons)	4105	4798	5506	3637
Trucks of livestock handled	51	54	52	52

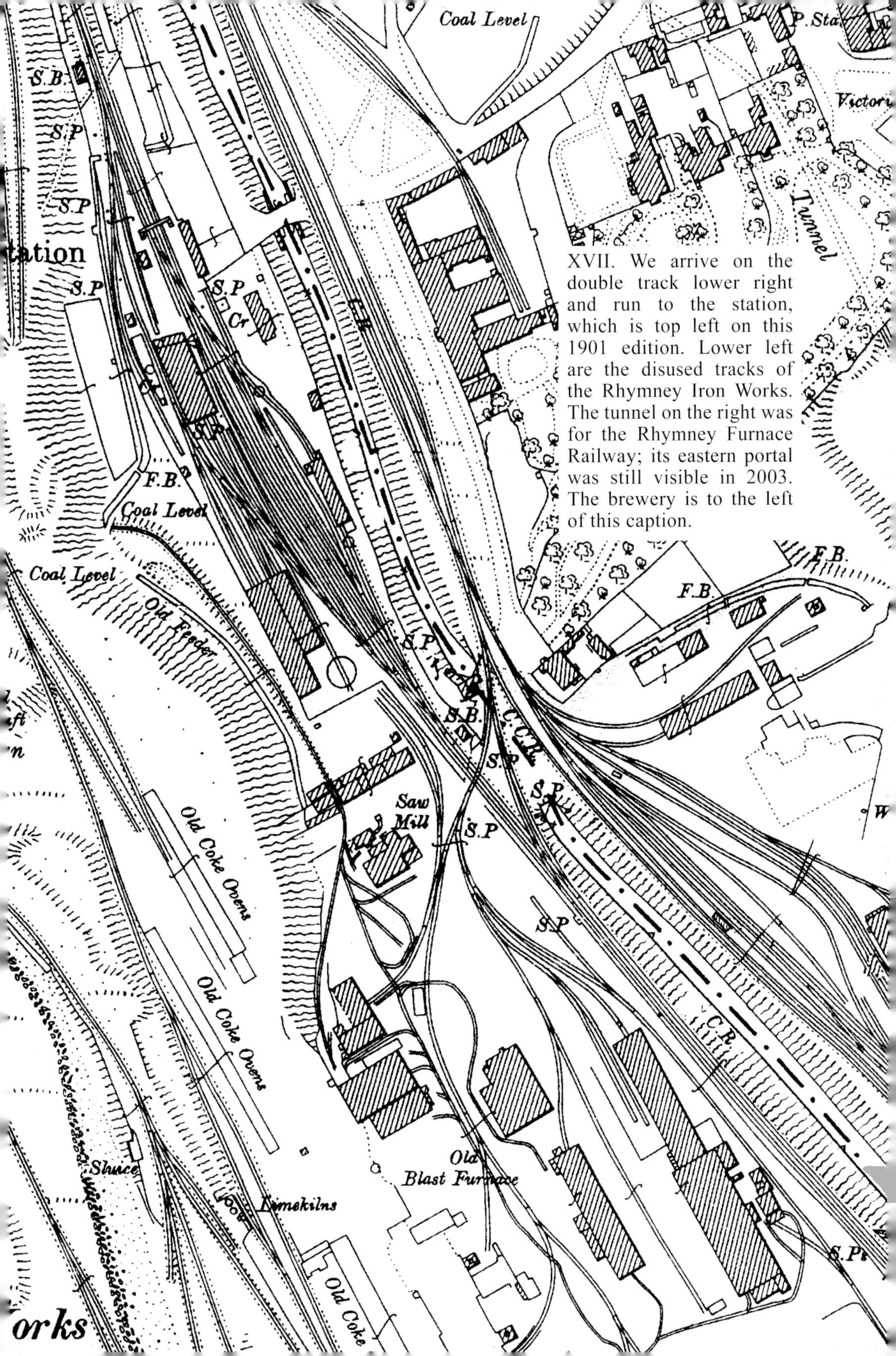

XVII. We arrive on the double track lower right and run to the station, which is top left on this 1901 edition. Lower left are the disused tracks of the Rhymney Iron Works. The tunnel on the right was for the Rhymney Furnace Railway; its eastern portal was still visible in 2003. The brewery is to the left of this caption.

60. There were 50 employees here in 1929-30, this reducing to 27 by 1938. A panorama across the town in about 1910 includes wagons standing on the tracks of the Rhymney Iron Company. The river is between them and the platforms. (Lens of Sutton coll.)

61. A 19th century view from near Rhymney Joint Signal Box has the goods yard framed by the footbridge. The platform on the right was used by a few Rhymney Bridge trains. South of here at this time were Rhymney Nos 1 and 2 signal boxes, and Rhymney (or Pontlottyn) Viaduct box. (LGRP)

62. The 3.50pm from Cardiff has just arrived behind 0-6-2T no. 5656 on 28th March 1948. The structure on the right is the coaling stage. (W.A.Camwell/SLS coll.)

63. No. 39 was an ex-RR 0-6-2T and was recorded in June 1949 wearing its new owner's temporary lettering. It seems that sister no. 78 is behind it. (P.Q.Treloar coll.)

64. As late as 18th July 1954, ex-RR coaches were still in use, albeit for workmen only. Two are in the old bay platform behind the engine shed. (P.J.Kelley)

65. The shed was recorded on 15th June 1963, as were nos 5622 and 6655. A loco and carriage loop line passes west of the building; its other end appears in pictures 61 and 62. Rain passes through the roof, hence the rafter shadows. (R.E.Toop/C.G.Maggs coll.)

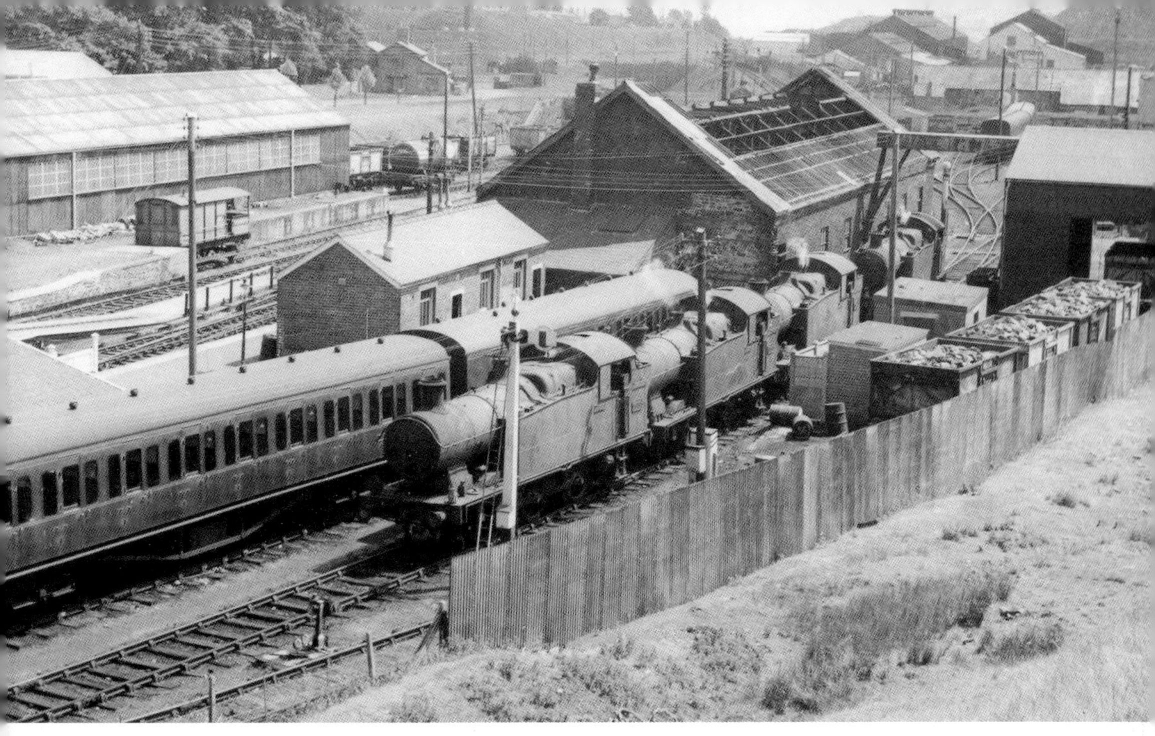

66. Another view on the same day includes nos 5605, 5666 and 5687, members of a popular class. In the distance is Maerdy Colliery and a massive tip. (R.E.Toop/C.G.Maggs coll.)

67. A diesel fuelling point was established north of the platforms. On the right is the 14.28 to Cardiff and the 14.56 waits in the background, but the date was not recorded. The operation was later transferred to Cardiff Canton Depot. (R.E.Toop/C.G.Maggs coll.)

68. Left of centre in this July 1966 panorama is the engine shed, which closed in March 1965. To the left of it is a new building for coaling. The signal box had a 61-lever frame, which was in use until 28th May 1972, having been brought into use on 22nd November 1936. (G.H.Tilt)

69. The north end of the new coal stage was pictured on 16th July 1967, with class 37s and a DMU in attendance. Nearest is no. D6874. (F.Hornby)

70. The corner of the 1925 goods shed is in the left background and complete in picture 66. Goods traffic ceased on 15th June 1964; a 6-ton crane was supplied in 1931. Distribution of coal began again in 1967. This photograph is from June 1968. (G.H.Tilt)

71. The up platform (right) was not used after 14th December 1969. It is seen on 10th September 1972, by which time the remaining sidings were only used for DMU stabling. (G.H.Tilt)

72. This September 1973 view makes an interesting comparison with picture 62. The up platform line had been lifted in the previous year. The redundant footbridge followed, but the loop line remained. (D.H.Mitchell)

73. A "Pacer" waits to bounce off to Penarth on 24th June 2003, wearing the Valley Lines logo. New platform paving gave a modernised ambiance. (B.I.Nathan)

74. A view in the other direction on 10th September 2003 reveals little of antiquity; it does not show that the environs have changed from black to green. The berthing sidings shown in picture 70 were still in use. Out of sight in the background were Reads's sidings, which carried tinplate traffic until about that time. (V.Mitchell)

75. The east elevation and the six-wheeled connecting bus to Tredegar were recorded on the same day. A visitor would not know of the intense industrial activity and pollution that once characterised this area. (V.Mitchell)

76. No. 33207 was recorded at dusk on 4th December 2005, the penultimate year of locomotive haulage on the route. The dark maroon livery was of West Coast Railways and sadly lacked contrasting lining. (P.Gray/M.J.Stretton coll.)

77. The location is seen again on 11th October 2008 after removal of the up platform and the recent completion of new berthing sidings, which could accommodate longer trains. Traffic figures were on the increase. (N.W.Sprinks)

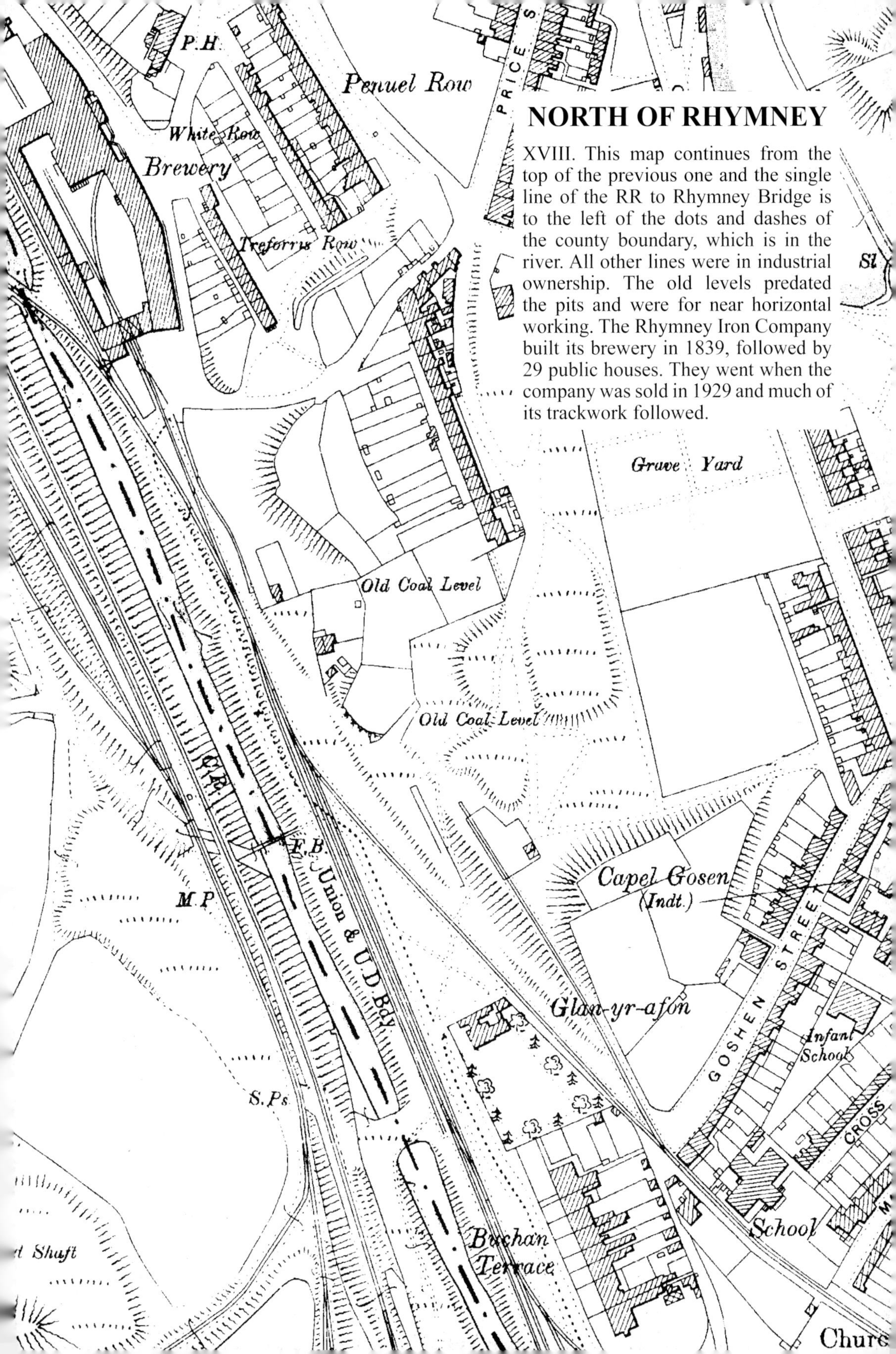

NORTH OF RHYMNEY

XVIII. This map continues from the top of the previous one and the single line of the RR to Rhymney Bridge is to the left of the dots and dashes of the county boundary, which is in the river. All other lines were in industrial ownership. The old levels predated the pits and were for near horizontal working. The Rhymney Iron Company built its brewery in 1839, followed by 29 public houses. They went when the company was sold in 1929 and much of its trackwork followed.

CEMETERY ROAD HALT

78. The location is a little over ½ mile north of Rhymney station and the stop was provided at the local council's request. It did not appear in timetables and was opened sometime after 1895. It had closed by 1928 and was built on the left. At the rear is an LNWR carriage on a through service. The RR coaches are in two-tone livery; this was replaced by a maroon brown in 1907. The loco is a K class 0-6-2T. (G.Davies coll.)

79. The halt was still evident in the early 1960s. The standard gauge tracks on the east side of the valley had ended behind the cottage in the centre of this eastward view.
(Frith & Co. postcard/G.Davies coll.)

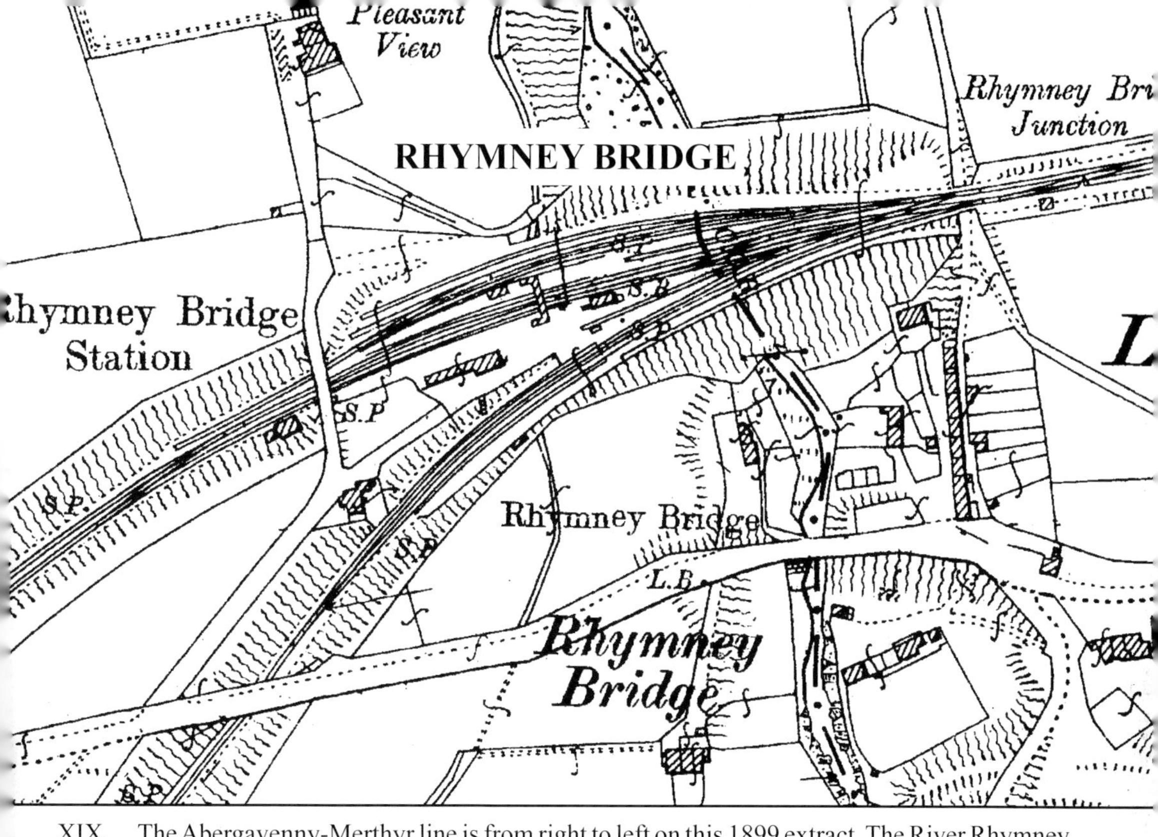

XIX. The Abergavenny-Merthyr line is from right to left on this 1899 extract. The River Rhymney flows from top to bottom and part of the village of Llechryd is on the right.

80. Another old photograph on offer is from 25th July 1922 and it shows RR 0-6-2ST no. 82 of 1897 on the north side of the station. The steam pump for its air brakes is on the side of the smokebox; it became GWR no. 117 and ran until about 1930. (R.S.Carpenter coll.)

81. A southward view from about 1935 features the two curved platforms for Rhymney trains, the nearest one normally being used. Llechryd is in the distance. (Stations UK)

Other views of this station are in *Abergavenny to Merthyr* in pictures 94-98.

82. The main line platforms are seen at about the same time, looking west. The connection to the loop is not shown on the map, but is visible beyond the bridge and is included on a diagram of 1890. Maybe this was a rare OS error. (Stations UK)

83. Ex-LNWR 0-8-0 no. 8924 departs east with ammonia tankers in tow on 26th April 1948. A train from Rhymney has arrived on the left and between it and the signal box is the short siding for local goods traffic. This ceased on 22nd November 1954. (W.S.Camwell/SLS coll.)

84. Photographed a few minutes later, ex-GWR 0-6-2T no. 5678 has run round its train and is ready to start the steep descent to Rhymney at 11.32am. (W.A.Camwell/SLS coll.)

85. This northward view was recorded in July 1958, seven months after the last passengers had travelled between Abergavenny and Merthyr. (H.C.Casserley)

86. All traffic was withdrawn on the line from Rhymney on 23rd September 1953 and freight on the east-west route ceased in late 1954. Demolition is in progress and all trace was lost under new highways, apart from the station house. It features in the previous picture. (W.A.Camwell/SLS coll.)

2. Pengam (Mon.) to New Tredegar

PENGAM (MON.)

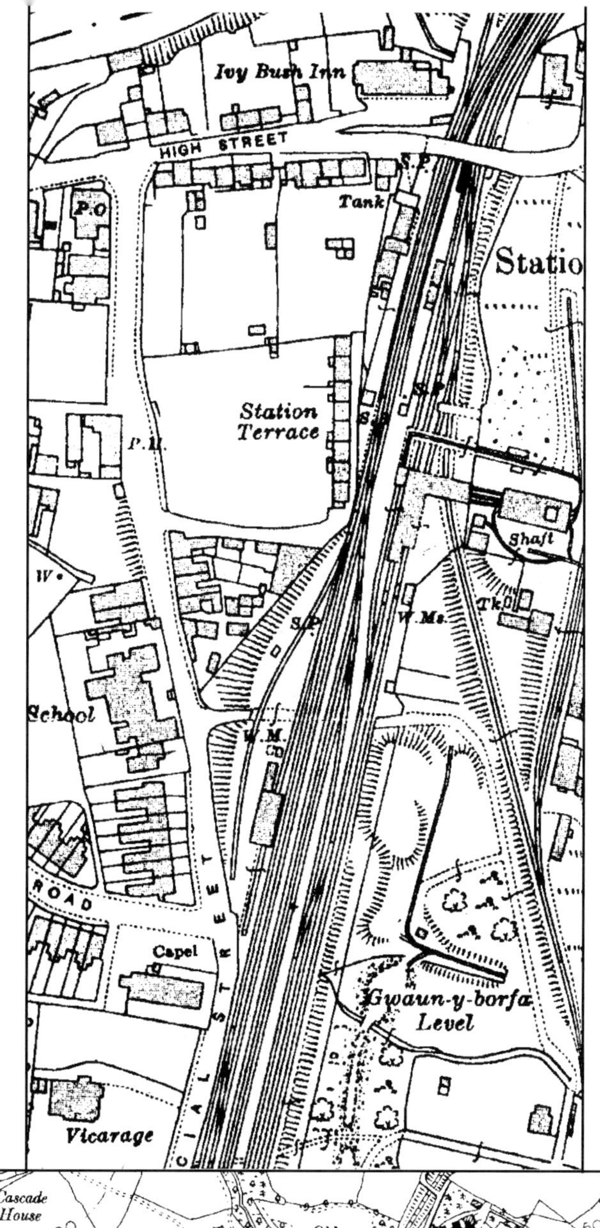

XX. The 1920 survey details the goods yard on the left; W.M. refers to Weighing Machine. On the right is part of the 1906 Pengam Colliery. Its access lines at the north pass east of the station and under the road. Production ceased in 1956.

XXI. The 1901 edition at 6ins to 1 mile includes both stations. Monmouthshire is to the right of the dots and dashes in the river. Britannia Colliery was later developed north of the station and Pengam Colliery south thereof. This part of the album is entirely on the former B&MR route.

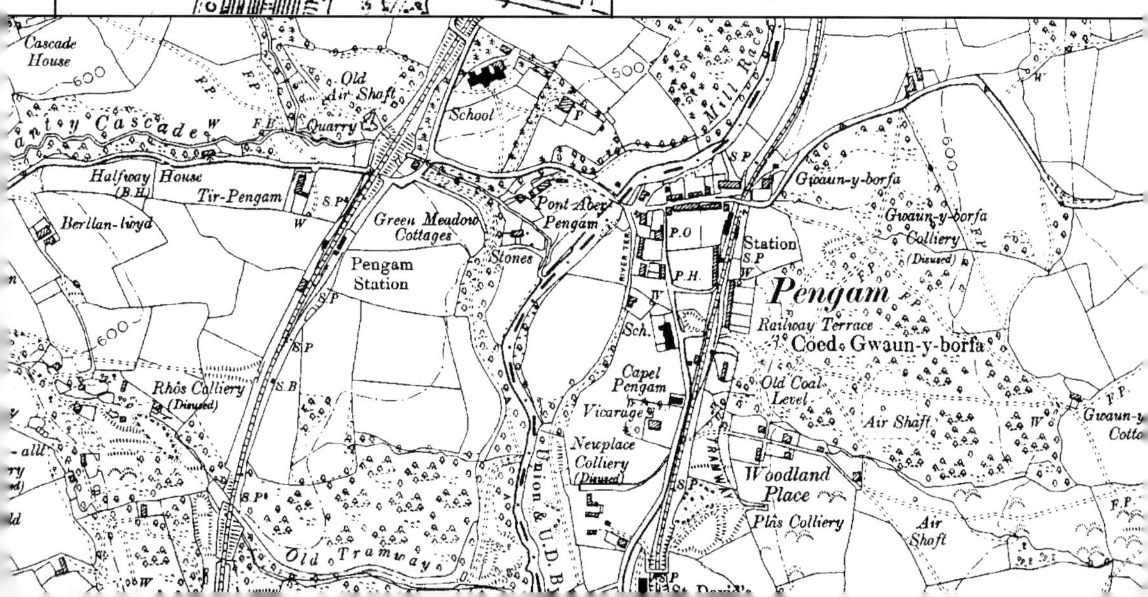

Other pictures of this location are numbered 84 to 87 in our *Brecon to Newport* album.

87. While a northbound 0-6-0PT takes refreshment in September 1960, we gain a glimpse of the 1915 Britannia Colliery and the line to it. Although this link was not used after 1958, the tracks north were retained until 1977 and coal ran via Bargoed Colliery. The route was singled in 1965. (D.K.Jones coll.)

88. Southbound with coal on the same day was 0-6-0PT no. 5758. The water column was close to the tank and the river was not far away as a source. The crossing was not for use by passengers; they were supposed to use the road bridge.
(D.K.Jones coll.)

89. Two pictures from 22nd August 1961 complete our survey. A connection to Pengam Colliery curves left; this link and the signal box were taken out of use on 6th July 1964. It was called Station box as there was also South, with 16 levers, and North, with 27. The latter closed at the same time; South in July 1934. (E.Wilmshurst)

90. "Pengam" became "Pengam & Fleur-de-Lis" on 1st February 1909, "Fleur-de-Lis" on 1st July 1924 and "Pengam (Mon)" on 29th March 1926. The 1.32pm to New Tredegar runs in behind 0-6-0PT no. 9664. Passenger services on both the routes ceased at the end of 1962. There had been a staff of 23 in 1923, but it had dropped to 8 by 1934. (E.Wilmshurst)

NORTH OF PENGAM

XXII. The 1901 edition at 6ins to 1 mile has our route and Aberbargoed Junction lower right. B&MR trains northbound diverged here, left for Brecon and right for New Tredegar. The latter ran close to Bargoed Colliery to reach Aberbargoed station (top). Bargoed station is marked "Junction". Bargoed Colliey Halt is not shown, as it did not open until about 1926. It does not show the 1904 Bargoed Pits Branch from the RR, which was in use until 1982.

BARGOED COLLIERY HALT

91. This part of the route had been singled in 1934 and the remaining platform was on the east side of the line. It was recorded in 1962. (Stations UK)

92. No. 36 approaches Bargoed Colliery on 7th March 1952, while its brake van is still on the up line. This is Bargoed Pits Junction on the former RR route and has already been seen in picture 29. It is shown here as this branch became the only link to the colliery after 1977. No. 36 was an 0-6-2T built by Hudswell Clarke for the RR in 1921. (S.Rickard/J&J coll.)

93. Working at the colliery in 1958 was ex-Barry Railway no. 133 carrying NCB 754 plates. The no. 754 had been attached by the GWR long before the loco was sold in the 1930s. (D.K.Jones coll.)

3133

2nd. SPECIAL SINGLE

Bargoed Colliery Halt to

(882)

PENGAM (MON)

(W) Fare 3d.

For Conditions see over

3133

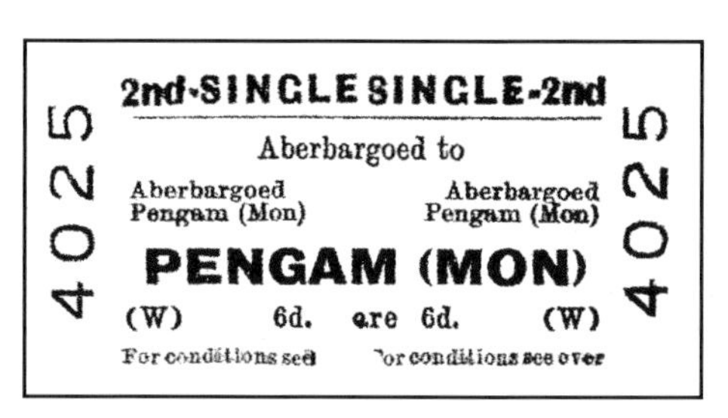

94. More of the aerial ropeway is to be seen as 0-6-2T no. 5244 couples up to a coal train in September 1960. The snap is from a train on the New Tredegar line. (D.K.Jones coll.)

95. A train for New Tredegar was captured across the colliery site at 3.10pm on 17th September 1962, the last year of its operation. The scenery was breathtaking for its awfulness. (R.E.Toop/C.G.Maggs coll.)

ABERBARGOED

96. The line was double from 1901 to 1934. This postcard is later, although there are still two platforms lower left. However, these were closed on 30th September 1935 and a new one was built. It can be seen inside the curve on the right. Bargoed Colliery and its tip are also on the right. There had been a goods yard with a shed, lower left, until 1935. (Lens of Sutton coll.)

97. No date or loco number exists, but it is certainly a down train and VIROL was still recommended. The gas lamps were of Suggs Windsor type. There were 18 men in 1923, but only one third of this number in 1931.(R.S.Carpenter coll.)

98. The remainder of the platform is included in this shot from 25th July 1959. At least the local council had updated to electric lighting. (A.M.Davies)

Aberbargoed	1923	1929	1930	1933
Passenger tickets issued	47366	17453	11704	16086
Season tickets issued	132	80	67	44
Parcels forwarded	2511	638	293	141
General goods forwarded (tons)	760	}		
Coal and coke received (tons)	347	}	Goods traffic included with Pengam (Glam) after 1926	
Other minerals received (tons)	1570	}		
General goods received (tons)	8399	}		
Trucks of livestock handled	-	}		

99. A 1962 record includes half the staff, three poster boards, four fire buckets and an open-topped gents, plus a gently smoking stove. All would soon be lost. (Stations UK)

100. A post-closure view suggests that there would be plenty of rest, but no travellers in future. The name evolved from "Aber Bargoed" to "Aber Bargoed & Bargoed" in 1905 to Bargoed & Aberbargoed" in 1909 and finally to "Aberbargoed" in 1924. (Stations UK)

CWMSYFIOG COLLIERY HALT

101. This was a public station when both platforms came into use in 1908 and it was named "Cwmsyfiog & Brithdir". The suffix was dropped on 1st July 1924 and from 5th July 1937 it was for colliers use only, as the platform shown in pictures 103-105 was then opened for the public. This photograph is from 1958 and has evidence of the former up platform on the right. There had been two signal boxes called Elliot Pit Junction between 1885 and 1934. The first had 11 levers and the second 23. (Stations UK)

Cwmsyfiog	1923	1929	1930	1933
Passenger tickets issued	34314	19955	17238	21965
Season tickets issued	47	63	60	9
Parcels forwarded	625	805	599	523

CWMSYFIOG HALT

102. A panorama from the Edwardian era features miners coaching stock berthed near the site of the future station, seen in the next pictures. The signal box is on the left; it is near the Queen Victoria Hotel on the next map. The carriages carry the letters PD for Powell Dyffryn. (G.Davies coll.)

103. Workers terraces and wonderless tips typify this often windy terrain. No.9488 coasts downhill with the 4.5pm New Tredegar to Newport train on 13th October 1962. (G.Daniels/R.M.Casserley coll.)

104. Arriving in 1962 we can observe electric lighting, rotten boarding and Monday's washing. The crowds of miners had shrunk to one man. There were two employed on the station in the 1930s. (Stations UK)

105. Departing moments later, observations include traditional seating, a ground frame hut and the south end of Elliot Colliery South Sidings. (Stations UK)

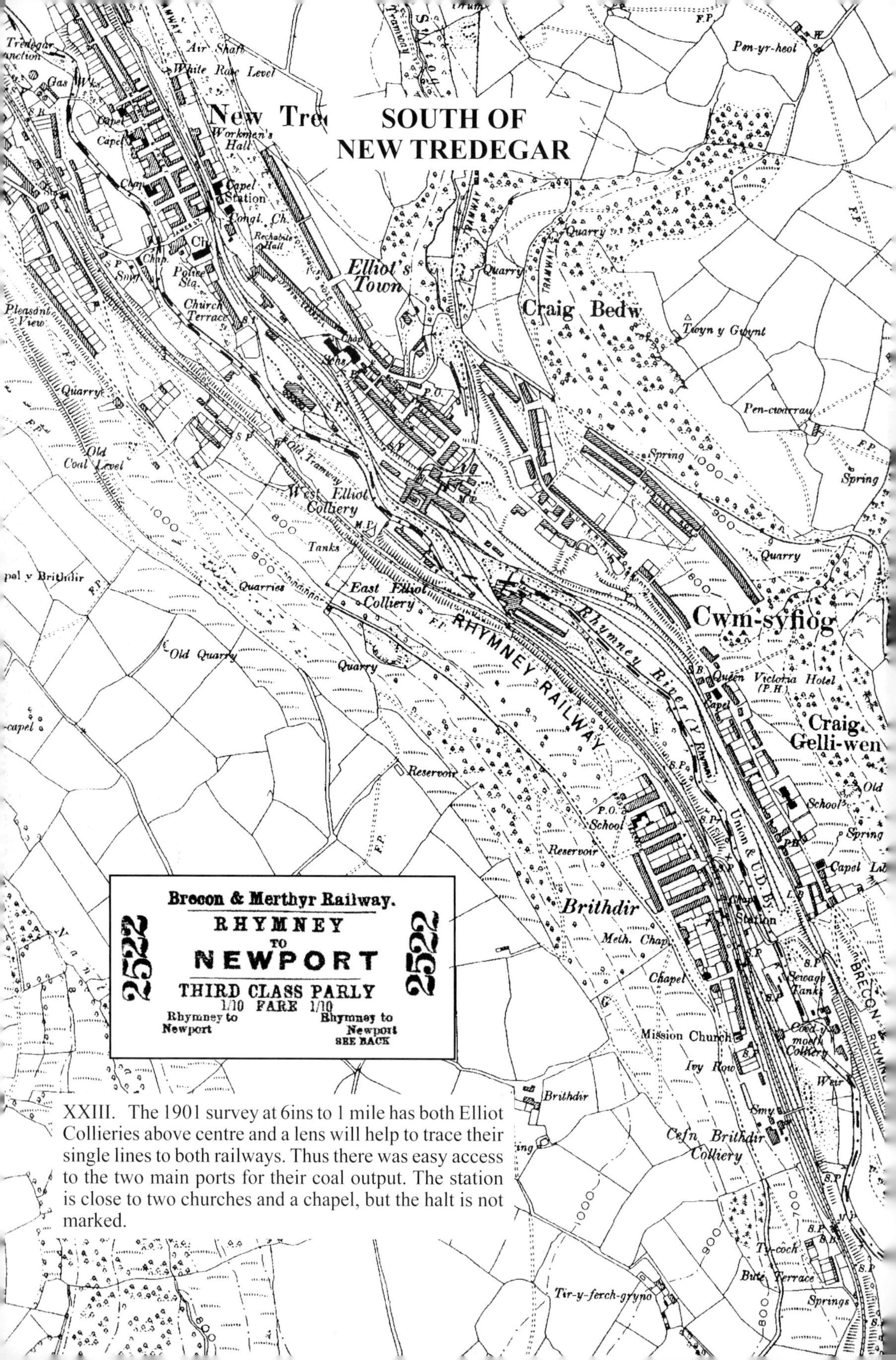

XXIII. The 1901 survey at 6ins to 1 mile has both Elliot Collieries above centre and a lens will help to trace their single lines to both railways. Thus there was easy access to the two main ports for their coal output. The station is close to two churches and a chapel, but the halt is not marked.

ELLIOT PIT HALT

106. The West Elliot Colliery was owned by Powell Duffryn, hence the PD wagons. The southern pit operated from 1883 to 1967. (A.Dudman coll.)

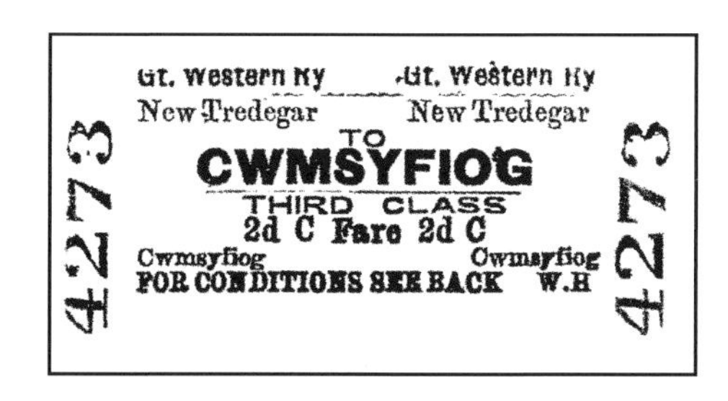

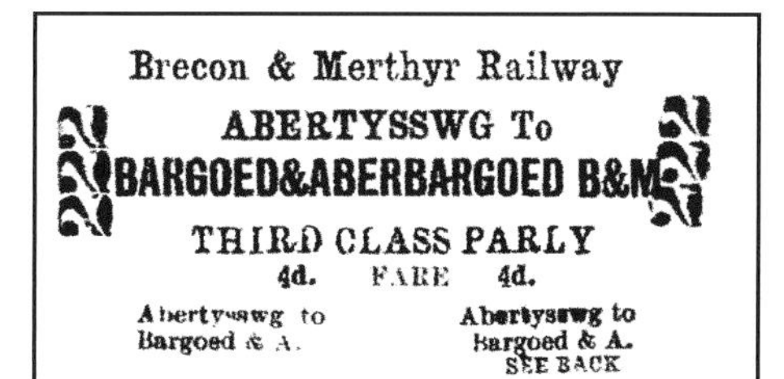

107. A glimpse from a passing up train in 1962 includes the pit head. Sinking of the first shaft had begun in 1883 and by 1912 over 2800 men were employed. Often one million tons of coal was raised annually, but closure came in 1967, when it was down to 0.5m. The site is now a mining museum. (Stations UK)

108. Looking south from the same train, the relics of a dying industry were on show to the occasional passing passenger. The halt was in use by 1926 for miners and was available until line closure. One example departs. (Stations UK)

NEW TREDEGAR

XXIV. The station is on the right and the RR is lower left on this 1901 survey. New Tredegar Colliery was started in 1853 with two shafts. Two more were sunk around 1905. Closure followed a landslide in 1929.

109. Initially the station was called "White Rose". It was "New Tredegar & White Rose" from 1885 until 1906 when it became "New Tredegar & Tirphil". The suffix was dropped in 1924. This southward view is from 1922. (D.K.Jones coll.)

➔ 110. Having just arrived at the up platform (right) no. 8495 darkens the washing slightly as it runs round its train on 25th July 1958. Evidence is present that its journey covered 18½ miles from Bassaleg Junction. (G.Adams/M.J.Stretton coll.)

➔ 111. Minutes later no. 8495 has been recoupled and this enables us to see the siding and almost to the end of the line. The route northwards closed on 14th April 1930. The siding had earlier served a coal level. (G.Adams/M.J.Stretton coll.)

New Tredegar	1923	1929	1930	1933
Passenger tickets issued	378729	270979	239730	29961
Season tickets issued	238	59	39	33
Parcels forwarded	12498	6074	5910	7258
General goods forwarded (tons)	280	}		
Coal and coke received (tons)	3604	}		
Other minerals received (tons)	1863	}	Not available	
General goods received (tons)	9905	}		
Trucks of livestock handled	1	}		

8495

NEW TREDEGAR

112. Chapels abound as we look south in 1958. On the left are Coke Oven Sidings and diverging on the right are Elliot Colliery North Sidings. There were 13 men here when the GWR took over, this being reduced to 6 by 1934. (Stations UK)

➔ 113. A fine finial is evident as a down train waits to leave on an unrecorded date. The box was in use from 18th July 1931 until line closure on the last day of 1962. The first box had 18 levers; this had 30. (W.A.Camwell/SLS coll.)

➔ 114. No. 9482 is leaving for Newport at 10.52am on 10th July 1958. Most roads on the sides of the valleys were as steep as James Street. (H.C.Casserley)

115. The line south had been singled beyond the wagons shown in picture 112 on 9th April 1934. A Newport train is about to use it on 25th July 1959 as we examine a Suggs Rochester pattern gas lamp. This gave shadow-free lighting. (A.M.Davies)

116. Tips are in view again as we look towards the end of the branch in September 1960. No. 3772 is an 0-6-0PT and it is about to run round its train. The signal would have seldom had a train to protect. (D.K.Jones coll.)

NEW TREDEGAR COLLIERY HALT

117. The up platform is on the left, but the down one is under rubble caused by a landslide in April 1930. There had been earlier falls in September 1928 and April 1929, but this one meant permanent closure of this part of the route. The fault runs across the valley and was the reason for the temporary branch closure in 2008, mentioned earlier.(GWR)

ABERTYSSWG

118. The station opened on 1st August 1905 and this view is probably soon after, from the north. In the background is the Tredegar Iron & Coal Company's MacLaren Colliery (No. 1 Pit), its miners platform and also the train for its workers. Out of view is the 30-lever signal box, which was in use from 1901 until line closure in 1930. (D.K.Jones coll.)

RHYMNEY LOWER

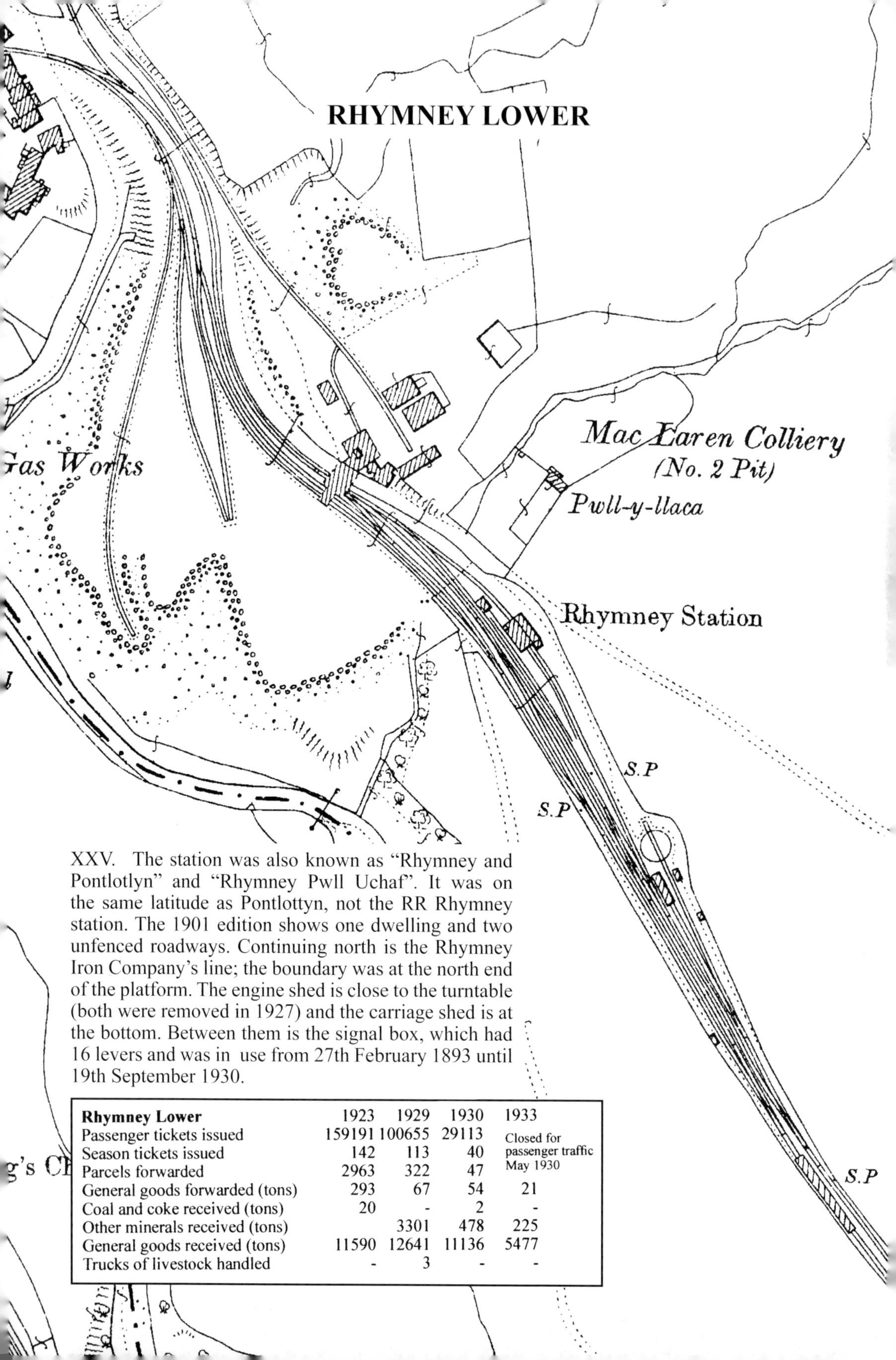

XXV. The station was also known as "Rhymney and Pontlotlyn" and "Rhymney Pwll Uchaf". It was on the same latitude as Pontlottyn, not the RR Rhymney station. The 1901 edition shows one dwelling and two unfenced roadways. Continuing north is the Rhymney Iron Company's line; the boundary was at the north end of the platform. The engine shed is close to the turntable (both were removed in 1927) and the carriage shed is at the bottom. Between them is the signal box, which had 16 levers and was in use from 27th February 1893 until 19th September 1930.

Rhymney Lower	1923	1929	1930	1933
Passenger tickets issued	159191	100655	29113	Closed for passenger traffic May 1930
Season tickets issued	142	113	40	
Parcels forwarded	2963	322	47	
General goods forwarded (tons)	293	67	54	21
Coal and coke received (tons)	20	-	2	-
Other minerals received (tons)		3301	478	225
General goods received (tons)	11590	12641	11136	5477
Trucks of livestock handled	-	3	-	-

119. The goods shed and goods office are painted black and the collieries are in the background in this 1922 panorama. The boundary gates and the water tank are included. There was a staff of 17 in 1923, but only one after 1930. (D.K.Jones coll.)

120. The site was recorded looking north in July 1935. Although the northern extremity closed to all traffic on 14th April 1930. MacLarens continued to be served until 12th November 1976 by the cross-valley link as mentioned in caption no. 51, at Tirphil. The area has now largely returned to a "green and pleasant land". (W.A.Camwell/SLS coll.)

Easebourne Lane, Midhurst, West Sussex.
GU29 9AZ Tel:01730 813169
www.middletonpress.co.uk email:info@middletonpress.co.uk

A-978 0 906520 B- 978 1 873793 C- 978 1 901706 D-978 1 904474 E - 978 1 906008

OOP Out of print at time of printing - Please check availability BROCHURE AVAILABLE SHOWING NEW TITLES

A
Abergavenny to Merthyr C 91 8
Abertillery and Ebbw Vale Lines D 84 5
Aldgate & Stepney Tramways B 70 1
Allhallows - Branch Line to A 62 8
Alton - Branch Lines to A 11 6
Andover to Southampton A 82 6
Ascot - Branch Lines around A 64 2
Ashburton - Branch Line to B 95 4
Ashford - Steam to Eurostar B 67 1
Ashford to Dover A 48 2
Austrian Narrow Gauge D 04 3
Avonmouth - BL around D 42 5
Aylesbury to Rugby D 91 3
B
Baker Street to Uxbridge D 90 6
Banbury to Birmingham D 27 2
Barking to Southend C 80 2
Barnet & Finchley Tramways B 93 0
Barry - Branch Lines around D 50 0
Bath Green Park to Bristol C 36 9
Bath to Evercreech Junction A 60 4
Bath Tramways B 86 2
Battle over Portsmouth 1940 A 29 1
Battle over Sussex 1940 A 79 6
Bedford to Wellingborough D 31 9
Betwixt Petersfield & Midhurst A 94 9
Birmingham to Wolverhampton E 25 3
Birmingham Trolleybuses E 19 2
Blackpool Tramways 1933-66 E 34 5
Bletchley to Cambridge D 94 4
Bletchley to Rugby E 07 9
Blitz over Sussex 1941-42 B 35 0
Bodmin - Branch Lines around B 83 1
Bognor at War 1939-45 B 59 6
Bombers over Sussex 1943-45 B 51 0
Bournemouth & Poole Trys B 47 3
Bournemouth to Evercreech Jn A 46 8
Bournemouth to Weymouth A 57 4
Bournemouth Trolleybuses C 10 9
Bradford Trolleybuses D 19 7
Brecon to Neath D 43 2
Brecon to Newport D 16 6
Brecon to Newtown E 06 2
Brighton to Eastbourne A 16 1
Brighton to Worthing A 03 1
Brighton Trolleybuses D 34 0
Bristols Tramways B 57 2
Bristol to Taunton D 03 6
Bromley South to Rochester B 23 7
Bromsgrove to Birmingham D 87 6
Bromsgrove to Gloucester D 73 9
Brunel - A railtour of his achievements D 74 6
Bude - Branch Line to B 29 9
Burnham to Evercreech Jn A 68 0
Burton & Ashby Tramways C 51 2
C
Camberwell & West Norwood Tys B 22 0
Cambridge to Ely D 55 5
Canterbury - Branch Lines around B 58 9
Cardiff to Dowlais (Cae Harris) E47 5
Cardiff to Swansea E 42 0
Cardiff Trolleybuses D 64 7
Caterham & Tattenham Corner B 25 1
Changing Midhurst C 15 4
Chard and Yeovil - BLs around C 30 7
Charing Cross to Dartford A 75 8
Charing Cross to Orpington A 96 3
Cheddar - Branch Line to B 90 9
Cheltenham to Andover C 43 7
Cheltenham to Redditch D 81 4
Chesterfield Tramways D 37 1
Chesterfield Trolleybuses D 51 7
Chester Tramways E 04 8
Chichester to Portsmouth A 14 7
Clapham & Streatham Trys B 97 8
Clapham Junction to Beckenham Jn B 36 7
Cleobury Mortimer - BLs around E 18 5
Clevedon & Portishead - BLs to D 18 0
Collectors Trains, Trolleys & Trams D 29 6
Colonel Stephens D62 3
Cornwall Narrow Gauge D 56 2
Cowdray & Easebourne D 96 8
Craven Arms to Llandeilo E 35 2
Crawley to Littlehampton A 34 5
Cromer - Branch Lines around C 26 0
Croydons Tramways B 42 8
Croydons Trolleybuses B 73 2
Croydon to East Grinstead B 48 0
Crystal Palace (HL) & Catford Loop A 87 1
Cyprus Narrow Gauge E13 0
D
Darlington - Leamside - Newcastle E 28 4
Darlington to Newcastle D 98 2
Darlington Trolleybuses D 33 3
Dartford to Sittingbourne B 34 3
Derby Tramways D 17 3
Derby Trolleybuses C 72 7
Derwent Valley - Branch Line to the D 06 7
Devon Narrow Gauge E 09 3
Didcot to Banbury D 02 9
Didcot to Swindon C 84 0
Didcot to Winchester C 13 0
Dorset & Somerset Narrow Gauge D 76 0
Douglas to Peel C 88 8
Douglas to Port Erin C 55 0
Douglas to Ramsey D 39 5
Dovers Tramways B 24 4
Dover to Ramsgate A 78 9
Dublin Northwards in the 1950s
Dunstable - Branch Lines to E 27 7
E
Ealing to Slough C 42 0
East Cornwall Mineral Railways D 22 7
East Croydon to Three Bridges A 53 6
East Grinstead - Branch Lines to A 07 9
East Ham & West Ham Tramways B 52 7
East London - Branch Lines of C 44 4
East London Line B 80 0
East Ridings Secret Resistance D 21 0
Edgware & Willesden Tramways C 18 5
Effingham Junction - BLs around A 74 1
Ely to Norwich C 90 1
Embankment & Waterloo Tramways B 41 1
Enfield Town & Palace Gates - BL to D 32 6
Epsom to Horsham A 30 7
Eritrean Narrow Gauge E 38 3
Euston to Harrow & Wealdstone C 89 5
Exeter & Taunton Tramways B 32 9
Exeter to Barnstaple B 15 2
Exeter to Newton Abbot C 49 9
Exeter to Tavistock B 69 5
Exmouth - Branch Lines to B 00 8
F
Fairford - Branch Line to A 52 9
Falmouth, Helston & St. Ives - BL to C 74 1
Fareham to Salisbury A 67 3
Faversham to Dover B 05 3
Felixstowe & Aldeburgh - BL to D 20 3
Fenchurch Street to Barking C 20 8
Festiniog - 50 yrs of enterprise C 83 3
Festiniog 1946-55 E 01 7
Festiniog in the Fifties B 68 8
Festiniog in the Sixties B 91 6
Frome to Bristol B 77 0
Fulwell - Trams, Trolleys & Buses D 11 1
G
Gloucester to Bristol D 35 7
Gloucester to Cardiff D 66 1
Gosport & Horndean Trys B 92 3
Gosport - Branch Lines around A 36 9
Great Yarmouth Tramways D 13 5
Greece Narrow Gauge D 72 2
Grimsby & Cleethorpes Trolleybuses D 86 9
H
Hammersmith & Hounslow Trys C 33 8
Hampshire Narrow Gauge D 36 4
Hampstead & Highgate Tramways B 53 4
Harrow to Watford D 14 2
Hastings to Ashford A 37 6
Hastings Tramways B 18 3
Hawkhurst - Branch Line to A 66 6
Hay-on-Wye - Branch Lines around D 92 0
Hayling - Branch Line to A 12 3
Haywards Heath to Seaford A 28 4
Hemel Hempstead - Branch Lines to D 88 3
Henley, Windsor & Marlow - BL to C77 2
Hereford to Newport D 54 8
Hexham to Carlisle D 75 3
Hitchin to Peterborough D 07 4
Holborn & Finsbury Tramways B 79 4
Holborn Viaduct to Lewisham A 81 9
Horsham - Branch Lines to A 02 4
Huddersfield Tramways D 95 1
Huddersfield Trolleybuses C 92 5
Hull Tramways D60 9
Hull Trolleybuses D 24 1
Huntingdon - Branch Lines around A 93 2
I
Ilford & Barking Tramways B 61 9
Ilford to Shenfield C 97 0
Ilfracombe - Branch Line to B 21 3
Ilkeston & Glossop Tramways D 40 1
Index to Middleton Press Stations E 24 6
Industrial Rlys of the South East A 09 3
Ipswich to Saxmundham C 41 3
Ipswich Trolleybuses D 59 3
Isle of Wight Lines - 50 yrs C 12 3
K
Keighley Tramways & Trolleybuses D 83 8
Kent & East Sussex Waterways A 72 X
Kent Narrow Gauge C 45 1
Kent Seaways - Hoys to Hovercraft D 79 1
Kidderminster to Shrewsbury E10 9
Kingsbridge - Branch Line to C 98 7
Kingston & Hounslow Loops A 83 3
Kingston & Wimbledon Tramways B 56 5
Kingswear - Branch Line to C 17 8
L
Lambourn - Branch Line to C 70 3
Launceston & Princetown - BL to C 19 2
Lewisham to Dartford A 92 5
Lines around Wimbledon B 75 6
Liverpool Street to Chingford D 01 2
Liverpool Street to Ilford C 34 5
Liverpool Tramways - Eastern C 04 8
Liverpool Tramways - Northern C 46 8
Liverpool Tramways - Southern C 23 9
Llandeilo to Swansea E 46 8
Llandudno & Colwyn Bay Tramways E 17 8
London Bridge to Addiscombe B 20 6
London Bridge to East Croydon A 58 1
London Termini - Past and Proposed D 00 5
London to Portsmouth Waterways B 43 5
Longmoor - Branch Lines to A 41 3
Looe - Branch Line to C 22 2
Lowestoft - Branch Lines around E 40 6
Ludlow to Hereford E 14 7
Lydney - Branch Lines around E 26 0
Lyme Regis - Branch Line to A 45 1
Lynton - Branch Line to B 04 6
M
Maidstone & Chatham Tramways B 40 4
March - Branch Lines around B 09 1
Margate & Ramsgate Tramways C 52 9
Marylebone to Rickmansworth D49 4
Melton Constable to Yarmouth Beach E 03 1
Mexborough to Swinton E 36 9
Midhurst - Branch Lines around A 49 9
Military Defence of West Sussex A 23 9
Military Signals, South Coast C 54 3
Mitcham Junction Lines B 01 5
Mitchell & company C 59 8
Monmouth - Branch Lines to E 20 8
Monmouthshire Eastern Valleys D 71 5
Moreton-in-Marsh to Worcester D 26 5
Moretonhampstead - BL to C 27 7
Mountain Ash to Neath D 80 7
N
Newbury to Westbury C 66 6
Newcastle to Hexham D 69 2
Newcastle Trolleybuses D 78 4
Newport (IOW) - Branch Lines to A 26 0
Newquay - Branch Lines to C 71 0
Newton Abbot to Plymouth C 60 4
Newtown to Aberystwyth E 41 3
Northern France Narrow Gauge C 75 8
North East German Narrow Gauge D 44 9
North Kent Tramways B 44 2
North London Line B 94 7
North Woolwich - BLs around C 65 9
Norwich Tramways C 40 6
Nottinghamshire & Derbyshire T/B D 63 0
Nottinghamshire & Derbyshire T/W D 53 1
O
Ongar - Branch Lines to E 05 5
Oxford to Bletchley D57 9
Oxford to Moreton-in-Marsh D 15 9
P
Paddington to Ealing C 37 6
Paddington to Princes Risborough C 81 9
Padstow - Branch Line to B 54 1
Peterborough to Kings Lynn
Plymouth - BLs around B 98 5
Plymouth to St. Austell C 63 5
Pontypool to Mountain Ash D 65 4
Porthmadog 1954-94 - BL around B 31 2
Portmadoc 1923-46 - BL around B 13 8
Portsmouths Tramways B 72 5
Portsmouth to Southampton A 31 4
Potters Bar to Cambridge D 70 8
Princes Risborough - Branch Lines to D 05 0
Princes Risborough to Banbury C 85 7
R
Reading to Basingstoke B 27 5
Reading to Didcot C 79 6
Reading to Guildford A 47 5
Reading Tramways B 87 9
Reading Trolleybuses C 05 5
Redhill to Ashford A 73 4
Return to Blaenau 1970-82 C 64 2
Rhymney and New Tredegar Lines E48 2
Rickmansworth to Aylesbury D 61 6
Romania & Bulgaria Narrow Gauge E 23 9
Roman Roads of Hampshire D 67 8
Roman Roads of Kent E 02 4
Roman Roads of Surrey C 61 1
Roman Roads of Sussex C 48 2
Romneyrail C 32 1
Ross-on-Wye - Branch Lines around E 30 7
Rugby to Birmingham E 37 6
Ryde to Ventnor A 19 2
S
Salisbury to Westbury B 39 8
Saxmundham to Yarmouth C 69 7
Saxony Narrow Gauge D 47 0
Scarborough Tramways E 15 4
Seaton & Eastbourne Tramways B 76 3
Seaton & Sidmouth - Branch Lines to A 95
Secret Sussex Resistance B 82 4
Selsey - Branch Line to A 04 8
Shepherds Bush to Uxbridge T/Ws C 28 4
Shrewsbury - Branch Line to A 86 4
Shrewsbury to Ludlow E 21 5
Shrewsbury to Newtown E 29 1
Sierra Leone Narrow Gauge D 28 9
Sirhowy Valley Line E 12 3
Sittingbourne to Ramsgate A 90 1
Slough to Newbury C 56 7
Solent - Creeks, Crafts & Cargoes D 52 4
Southamptons Tramways B 33 6
Southampton to Bournemouth A 42 0
Southend-on-Sea Tramways B 28 2
Southern France Narrow Gauge C 47 5
Southwark & Deptford Tramways B 38 1
South W Harbours - Ships & Trades E 22 2
Southwold - Branch Line to A 15 4
South London Line B 46 6
South London Tramways 1903-33 D 10 4
South London Tramways 1933-52 D 89 0
South Shields Trolleybuses E 11 6
St. Albans to Bedford D 08 1
St. Austell to Penzance C 67 3
Stourbridge to Wolverhampton E 16 1
St. Pancras to Barking D 68 5
St. Pancras to St. Albans C 78 9
Stamford Hill Tramways B 85 5
Steaming through the Isle of Wight A 56 7
Steaming through West Hants A 69 7
Stratford upon avon to Birmingham D 77
Stratford upon Avon to Cheltenham C 25
Surrey Home Guard C 57 4
Surrey Narrow Gauge C 87 1
Sussex Home Guard C 24 6
Sussex Narrow Gauge C 68 0
Swanley to Ashford B 45 9
Swindon to Bristol C 96 3
Swindon to Gloucester D46 3
Swindon to Newport D 30 2
Swiss Narrow Gauge C 94 9
T
Talyllyn - 50 years C 39 0
Taunton to Barnstaple B 60 2
Taunton to Exeter C 82 6
Tavistock to Plymouth B 88 6
Tees-side Trolleybuses D 58 6
Tenterden - Branch Line to A 21 5
Three Bridges to Brighton A 35 2
Tilbury Loop C 86 4
Tiverton - Branch Lines around C 62 8
Tivetshall to Beccles D 41 8
Tonbridge to Hastings A 44 4
Torrington - Branch Lines to B 37 4
Towcester - Branch Lines around E 39 0
Trident Tankers Ltd E 43 7
Tunbridge Wells - Branch Lines to A 32 1
Twickenham & Kingston Trys C 35 2
U
Upwell - Branch Line to B 64 0
V
Victoria & Lambeth Tramways B 49 7
Victoria to Bromley South A 98 7
Vivarais Revisited E 08 6
W
Walthamstow & Leyton Tramways B 65 7
Waltham Cross & Edmonton Trys C 07 9
Wandsworth & Battersea Tramways B 63
Wantage - Branch Line to D 25 8
Wareham to Swanage - 50 yrs D 09 8
War on the Line A 10 9
Waterloo to Windsor A 54 3
Waterloo to Woking A 38 3
Watford to Leighton Buzzard D 45 6
Welshpool to Llanfair E 49 9
Wenford Bridge to Fowey C 09 3
Westbury to Bath B 55 8
Westbury to Taunton C 76 5
West Cornwall Mineral Railways D 48 7
West Croydon to Epsom B 08 4
West German Narrow Gauge D 93 7
West London - Branch Lines of C 50 5
West London Line B 84 8
West Wiltshire - Branch Lines of D 12 8
Weymouth - Branch Lines around A 65 9
Willesden Junction to Richmond B 71 8
Wimbledon to Beckenham C 58 1
Wimbledon to Epsom B 62 6
Wimborne - Branch Lines around A 97 0
Wisbech - Branch Lines around C 01 7
Wisbech 1800-1901 C 93 2
Woking to Alton A 59 8
Woking to Portsmouth A 25 3
Woking to Southampton A 55 0
Wolverhampton to Shrewsbury E 44 4
Wolverhampton Trolleybuses D 85 2
Woolwich & Dartford Trolleys B 66 4
Worcester to Birmingham D 97 5
Worcester to Hereford D 38 8
Worthing to Chichester A 06 2
Y
Yeovil - 50 yrs change C 38 3
Yeovil to Dorchester A 76 5
Yeovil to Exeter A 91 8
York Tramways & Trolleybuses D 82 1